ENDORSEMENTS

If you are a woman building a business, leading a family, and attempting to carry vision, responsibility, and leadership alone, this book is for you.

There are seasons when women don't need another strategy; they need reassurance. They need permission to slow down, re-center, and remember why they started in the first place. *Becoming SHE-EO* offers exactly that.

Page by page, this book calls women back to intimacy with God, clarity of purpose, and peace in the process. It's a beautiful companion for any woman who wants to grow spiritually while still honoring the dreams God placed in her heart.

Thank you, Karen, on behalf of the women who lead and pour out daily. This devotional feels like living water to a weary soul. We needed this.

Tresa Todd
Founder of Women's Real Estate Investors Network
Frisco, TX

Becoming SHE-EO anchored me in God's Word and clearly reaffirmed my calling to lead in obedience to Him. As Chief Operating Officer of Patriot Mobile, I am entrusted with stewarding a mission far bigger than business, and this 52-week devotional was both deeply inspirational and genuinely encouraging. Its thoughtful weekly format creates space for reflection, prayer, and renewed strength, keeping me grounded in truth amid full seasons of leadership. This book is a powerful resource for any woman who desires to pursue God's purpose for her life and lead others without compromising her faith, family, or values.

Jenny Story
Chief Operating Officer, Patriot Mobile LLC
Grapevine, TX

How exciting to endorse such a timely book designed with a powerful purpose for every woman. Whether you are leading a company, your family, or both, *Becoming SHE-EO* will impact your push and your pause. Karen Schatzline, once again, delivers an opportunity to draw closer to your Creator and fulfill all He has in store for you.

Joni Lamb
Daystar Television Network
Bedford, TX

Becoming SHE-EO is a thoughtfully and powerfully crafted 52-week devotional that invites women to lead from a place of deep faith, biblical truth, and God-given purpose. Through Scripture, reflection, prayer, and practical leadership insight, Karen Schatzline reminds readers that faith and leadership are not separate pursuits but a unified calling. This devotional speaks powerfully to women who are building businesses, nurturing families, and stewarding influence while keeping God at the center of it all. Having known Karen personally as a trusted friend and leader, I can attest that the wisdom, authenticity, and conviction found in these pages reflect the life she lives and the leadership she models every day. *Becoming SHE-EO* is an inspiring guide for women who desire to lead boldly, love deeply, and leave a legacy rooted in faith.

Emily Epperson
General Counsel, Patriot Mobile LLC
Fort Worth, TX

Karen did a beautiful job of elevating all women to reach new heights for Christ in *Becoming SHE-EO*. This book will leave you enthused and inspired to become all that God created you to be. It propels you to achieve the next level in your life and in God's purposes. You are guaranteed to find some area in your life that you want to improve and grow in. Also, to help others do the same. I couldn't wait to devour the contents of this book, and I guarantee the same for you, too. After you read and apply what you've learned, you will feel reignited. There will be resurrection power in your unfulfilled assignments and unanswered prayers. Your purpose, dreams, and destiny will become clearer and fueled with hope. I can't wait for this book to be published. I will be buying extras to give away. It is an honor to know Karen. I highly recommend that every woman read this devotional life guide. Leave a Legacy of Impact.

Teri Bailey
Author, Speaker, Co-Founder of
FlashPoint and FlashPoint Network
Newark, TX

Karen Schatzline is the real deal. She walks the walk in a way I rarely see, as a mom, wife, and businesswoman with conviction and consistency. She wrote *Becoming SHE-EO* for the woman building big things who refuses to sacrifice what matters most and is committed to divine order: God first, family second, business third. This devotional is powerful, practical, and packed with truth that will shift how you lead and live. If you want a weekly reset that realigns your heart and strengthens your faith, this belongs on your nightstand.

Ali Spitsbergen
Founder, For His Glory CEO
7-Figure Business Mentor and Podcast Host
San Marcos, CA

Becoming SHE-EO is more than a devotional; it's a transformational journey that calls women higher in both faith and leadership. Karen is a bright light, and her encouraging gifts are threaded throughout each biblical teaching, activation assignment, and affirmation. Her life is a living testimony of resilience, surrender, and unwavering obedience to God, which allows her voice on the pages to carry both authority and tenderness. This devotional doesn't just inspire, it awakens you to live a purpose-driven life, anchored in Christ while simultaneously building a legacy that truly matters.

Andrea Kaye Goodman
Investor and Entrepreneur
Tempe, AZ

If you sense that God has called you to build, lead, or steward something that matters, *Becoming SHE-EO* will meet you right where you are. Karen Schatzline is a wise and trusted teacher whose life reflects the truths she teaches—rooted in intimacy with God and lived with integrity. I'm proud to call her friend. This devotional thoughtfully guides you through identity, foundation, vision, leadership, resilience, and legacy, preparing you to build with God rather than striving on your own. As you move through these pages, you won't just be inspired—you'll be formed, strengthened, and equipped to steward what God has entrusted to you.

Brandie Barclay
Founder of PowerSoul Women's Ministry
Author of *POWERSOUL, Lit from Within*
Phoenix, AZ

In *Becoming SHE-EO – A Yearlong Devotional Life Guide,* Karen Schatzline provides a blueprint for success for every woman with a dream or vision. Karen, a real-life SHE-EO, has extended her hand, looked into our eyes, and said, "I will walk with you." The journey includes scripture, powerful devotions, prayer, journal prompts, and affirmations that strengthen leadership, expand influence, and align daily decisions with God's purpose. This transformative guide will shape a trailblazing legacy grounded in faith, rooted in courage, and multiplied by the Holy Spirit. This book is for you—and for those you influence!

Bettina "Tina" Richardson, J.D.
Retired Federal Prosecutor
Co-Pastor and International Speaker
Former District Women's Director, South Texas Network, Assemblies of God
San Antonio, TX

"Life is a great big adventure with God—embrace every part of the journey." This is a quote my mama, Karen Schatzline, has spoken over my life for as long as I can remember. She has taught me that as women, we are called to see life as one great adventure with God through every season—whether you're a young adult fresh out of college with entrepreneurial dreams, a mom balancing family and work, or someone learning that ministry and business can truly coexist.

This 52-week devotional, *Becoming SHE-EO*, is powerful, practical, and deeply inspiring. Every devotion reflects not only biblical truth, but the very heart of the woman my mama is and the example she has lived out daily. She has shaped me into the woman I am today by showing me that we don't have to second-guess the calling God has placed on our lives. Leadership, faith, family, business, and legacy are not competing roles—they go hand in hand.

If you are searching for permission to walk confidently in all that God has called you to be, this devotional will meet you right where you are.

Abby Schatzline
Entrepreneur and Social Media Manager
Southlake, TX

Karen Schatzline is a true pioneer of the faith, modeling what it looks like to live as a daughter of the King and lead with Kingdom authority. Through her life and leadership, she shows the Body of Christ how as women we carry both humility and influence. From global stages to everyday obedience, she has carried the Gospel with excellence and authority, speaking to thousands and leading countless hearts to Christ. Karen doesn't just speak the message. She lives it by modeling what it truly means to lead as a SHE-EO, and generations are impacted because of her yes.

Thea Wood
Author of *Kick Fear in the Face*
Scottsdale, AZ

Becoming SHE-EO speaks to women who are carrying influence and responsibility while longing to stay anchored in God and also enjoy the journey. Karen offers wisdom that is both deeply biblical and refreshingly honest, meeting readers in real life. This devotional invites women to lead from a place of strength, health, and spiritual depth rather than striving, burnout, or obligation. Much needed in today's world!

Megan Valentine
Author, Entrepreneur
Transformation Coach and Founder of Build Your Brave
Peoria, AZ

Becoming SHE-EO is not just inspiring, it's grounding for the woman who is leading, building, and carrying a lot with purpose. Karen beautifully captures what it looks like to pursue vision, family, and faith without living in burnout or constant striving. This devotional equips women to lead with wisdom, build with intention, and stay deeply rooted in God's presence as they grow in both calling and legacy. It's a powerful resource for any woman who knows she's created for more.

Bekah Tinter
Metabolic Health Strategist, Coach Developer
Co-Founder of She Leads Well
Gilbert, AZ
www.sheleadswell.net

As a pastor's wife and someone who has spent years walking alongside women in their faith journeys, I can confidently say that *Becoming SHE-EO* is a much-needed resource. This 52-week Bible study beautifully combines God's Word with practical application, helping women build strong faith while discovering their God-given destiny. It's not just inspiring—it's grounding, empowering, and life-giving. Resources like this are rare, and I believe my friend Karen has designed a resource that will become a trusted companion for women who are ready to grow spiritually and step into all God has called them to be.

Mary Alessi
Worship Artist and Co-Founder of Metro Life Church
Miami, FL

Karen is solid in the Word, deeply grounded in her faith, and she has truly lived the pages of this book. What she writes is not theory—it is truth forged through obedience, surrender, and seasons walked faithfully with God. Karen writes as a seasoned leader who knows how to lead with both strength and humility. This devotional will anchor you in God's Word while inviting you into a life of purpose, peace, and intimate leadership with Him. Get ready to become everything He created you to be.

Cathy Greer
Mentor, Coach, and President of Mission
Support Network, Vista, CA
www.msnministries.org
www.cathygreer.org

Becoming SHE-EO is a devotional written with passion and purpose—a purpose that calls each of us out of the ordinary and helps us understand, through the Word and with God, that all things are possible. This devotional will call you to arise, just as Esther did, and stand in your God-given authority, saying "Yes" to His call to chase your dream and leave changed lives in your wake.

Karen is a dear friend whose desire is to bring out the giant killer in each of us and to help us stand in God's strength so we can win. Her life bears the fruit of slaying giants, nurturing her family, and leaving a legacy everywhere she goes. Take the words of this devotional, apply them to your life, and boldly chase your dream!

Pastor Phyllis Sawyer
Co-Pastor, Calvary Assembly
Decatur, AL

Becoming SHE-EO reflects a journey I have seen lived out with faith, courage, and perseverance. In this devotional, Karen beautifully guides women through identity, inner growth, leadership, and lasting impact with honesty and wisdom. It will encourage women to trust the process of who they are becoming as they step boldly into their calling.

Adrienne Schatzline
Realtor, Elite Real Estate Texas
Fort Worth, TX

Becoming SHE-EO beautifully affirms the divine worth and spiritual potential of women. It guides us toward a deeper relationship with God and inspires us to live with greater purpose, faith, and confidence in our God-given role.

Allyson Chard
Non-Profit Builder & Community Activist
Gibson Island, MD

Credibility is a timeless gold standard for any weighty personal decision—as in the choice before you now, whether to invest your priceless time and resources in *Becoming SHE-EO*. I am a personal, decades-long witness that Karen Schatzline is a compelling writer whose extraordinary, biblically grounded life strategies are matched by an excellent spirit you can trust. She does not merely teach these principles—she lives them, standing as a living testimony to their effectiveness. Her counsel echoes the apostle Paul's exhortation in 1 Corinthians 11:1: "Be imitators of me, as I am of Christ," reminding us that we are His workmanship, created for good works prepared in advance for us to walk in. So yes—invest now, and be equipped to follow Karen's legacy of "leading boldly, loving deeply, and leaving a legacy."

Tava Brice
Women's Ministry Director and Co-Founder of Covenant Love Church
Fayetteville, NC

I'm already thinking about how I am implementing this devotional into my morning routine. Karen carefully weaves faith, motivation, and the Word into this beautiful book. I know her, and I know she daily lives out the promises this writing reveals. If you are rockin' that SHE-EO life or you want to believe you were made for more—you are going to be encouraged and grow!

Elizabeth Knowles
First Lady, Magnolia Region Church of God of Prophecy
Founder of www.morningmattersroutine.com
Terry, MS

Karen Schatzline sends out a clarion call to women to rise up and take hold of what God has built in you as a woman. Whatever stage of life you are in, *Becoming SHE-EO* will equip and empower you with God-given direction to be SHE-EO. It will inspire you to live out God's truth in your life!

Candace Manning
Spirit Life Pastor, Christian Life Center
Fort Lauderdale, FL

Having partnered with Karen Schatzline in both ministry and business for the last decade, I can say with confidence this devotional is the message she lives. *Becoming SHE-EO* reframes success through an eternal lens, reminding us that our work is about legacy, impact, and honoring God above all. It's a must-read for women leading with faith and vision.

Jen Jones
CEO and founder of The Significant Life
San Diego, CA

This 52-week devotional is a powerful encouragement for women who desire to grow in confidence and believe

God for more. My amazing friend, Karen Schatzline, beautifully shares God's promises while reminding us that we are capable, called, and equipped to accomplish the dreams God has placed in our hearts. Each week strengthens our faith, builds courage, and inspires us to walk forward with confidence and purpose. I have personally experienced the wonderful results of Karen Schatzline's leadership that continues to impact my life today.

This amazing book will help you believe that you are made for more and you can do all that God has called you to do! It is a powerful devotional that is so timely for women to rise up in boldness and walk in their divine destiny!

Diana Burks
Senior Pastor of Overflow Life Church
Keller, TX

Becoming SHE-EO is a powerful invitation to step into the woman God always designed you to be—old in faith, confident in purpose, and anchored in peace. Karen Schatzline reminds us that success and serenity are not opposites, but divine partners when God is at the center of our lives. This amazing devotional, written by my friend and mentor, will awaken your courage, strengthen your identity, and fill your journey with hope as you rise into your true calling as a SHE-EO.

Jennifer Curry
Wife, Mom, Mimi, Minister of the Gospel
Pensacola, FL

Becoming SHE-EO is a powerful and timely devotional for women who are building lives of purpose without abandoning their faith, families, or calling. This devotional is for the woman who knows she was created for more—but wants to build it God's way. *Becoming SHE-EO* offers steady, Scripture-rooted encouragement for leading boldly while staying deeply grounded. Karen doesn't just inspire—she anchors you in truth, wisdom, and spiritual clarity for the long haul. These pages will strengthen your faith, sharpen your vision, and remind you that your leadership matters to God. I'm deeply proud of this work and the woman who stewarded it so well.

Heather Wallace
Author and Speaker
Co-Pastor New Hope Worship Center
Grovetown, GA

BECOMING SHE-EO

BECOMING SHE-EO

A Yearlong Devotional Life Guide for Women Chasing Dreams, Nurturing Family, and Leaving a Legacy of Impact

KAREN SCHATZLINE

© Copyright 2026– Karen Schatzline

All rights reserved. This book is protected by the copyright laws of the United States of America. This book may not be copied or reprinted for commercial gain or profit. The use of short quotations or occasional page copying for personal or group study is permitted and encouraged. Permission will be granted upon request. Scripture quotations marked NKJV are taken from the New King James Version. Copyright © 1982 by Thomas Nelson, Inc. Used by permission. All rights reserved. Scripture quotations marked AMP are taken from the Amplified® Bible, Copyright © 2015 by The Lockman Foundation, La Habra, CA 90631. All rights reserved. Used by permission. Scripture quotations marked KJV are taken from the King James Version. Scripture quotations marked TPT are taken from *The Passion Translation*, Copyright © 2017, 2018, 2020 by Passion & Fire Ministries, Inc., www.thepassiontranslation.com. Used by permission of BroadStreet Publishing Group, LLC, Racine, Wisconsin, USA. All rights reserved. Scripture quotations marked ESV are taken from The Holy Bible, English Standard Version® (ESV®), copyright © 2001 by Crossway, a publishing ministry of Good News Publishers. Used by permission. All rights reserved. Scripture quotations marked NIV are taken from the HOLY BIBLE, NEW INTERNATIONAL VERSION®, Copyright © 1973, 1978, 1984, 2011 International Bible Society. Used by permission of Zondervan. All rights reserved. Scripture quotations marked NLT are taken from the Holy Bible, New Living Translation, copyright 1996, 2004, 2015. Used by permission of Tyndale House Publishers, Wheaton, Illinois 60189. All rights reserved. Scripture quotations marked MSG are taken from *The Message*. Copyright © 1993, 1994, 1995, 1996, 2000, 2001, 2002. Used by permission of NavPress Publishing Group. Used by permission. All rights reserved. All emphasis within Scripture quotations is the author's own. Take note that the name satan and related names are not capitalized. We choose not to acknowledge him, even to the point of violating grammatical rules.

DESTINY IMAGE® PUBLISHERS, INC.
P.O. Box 310, Shippensburg, PA 17257-0310
"Publishing cutting-edge prophetic resources to supernaturally empower the body of Christ"

This book and all other Destiny Image and Destiny Image Fiction books are available at Christian bookstores and distributors worldwide.

For more information on foreign distributors, call 717-532-3040.
Reach us on the Internet: www.destinyimage.com.

ISBN 13 TP: 979-8-8815-0970-5
ISBN 13 eBook: 979-8-8815-0971-2

For Worldwide Distribution, Printed in the U.S.A.
1 2 3 4 5 6 7 8 / 30 29 28 27 26

DEDICATION

To every woman who has ever questioned her calling, doubted her voice, or underestimated the strength God placed within her—this devotional is for you.

To the daughters of God who dream, build, pioneer, worship, rise, and keep choosing obedience over fear: May these pages remind you that you are seen, known, chosen, and divinely equipped.

Your leadership matters. Your influence matters. Your legacy matters.

To the trailblazing SHE-EO women who went before me—thank you. Your courage, vision, and faithfulness paved the way, broke barriers, and created space for the next generation of women to rise. Your legacy inspires every page of this devotional.

To my amazing husband, Pat Schatzline, my son, Nate Schatzline, and grandsons, Jack and Andy—thank you for your unwavering love, support, and encouragement. Though this devotional is written for women, your belief in me and in my calling has made it possible to write it all. You have cheered me on, lifted me up, and celebrated every step of this journey.

Your presence reminds me that strength, courage, and leadership are nurtured not only by self but also by those who champion us along the way.

To my own legacy—my daughter, Abby Schatzline, and my daughter-in-love, Adrienne Schatzline, and my granddaughter, Skylar Schatzline (and those who may come in the future) brilliant SHE-EOs whose spirits shine with purpose and possibility: I am endlessly proud of each of you—for the women you are, the strength of your faith, the boldness of your dreams, and the integrity with which you pursue your calling.

Thank you for inspiring me, celebrating my victories, and now allowing me the joy of being your biggest cheerleader. I pray you always lead with love, rise with courage, create with conviction, and walk boldly in the identity God has stamped on your lives. May you feel God's whisper in your becoming, His strength in your steps, and His delight in every season you step into.

You were born for such a time as this. And the world is already brighter because of the women who came before, the people who support you along the way, and the extraordinary women you are becoming.

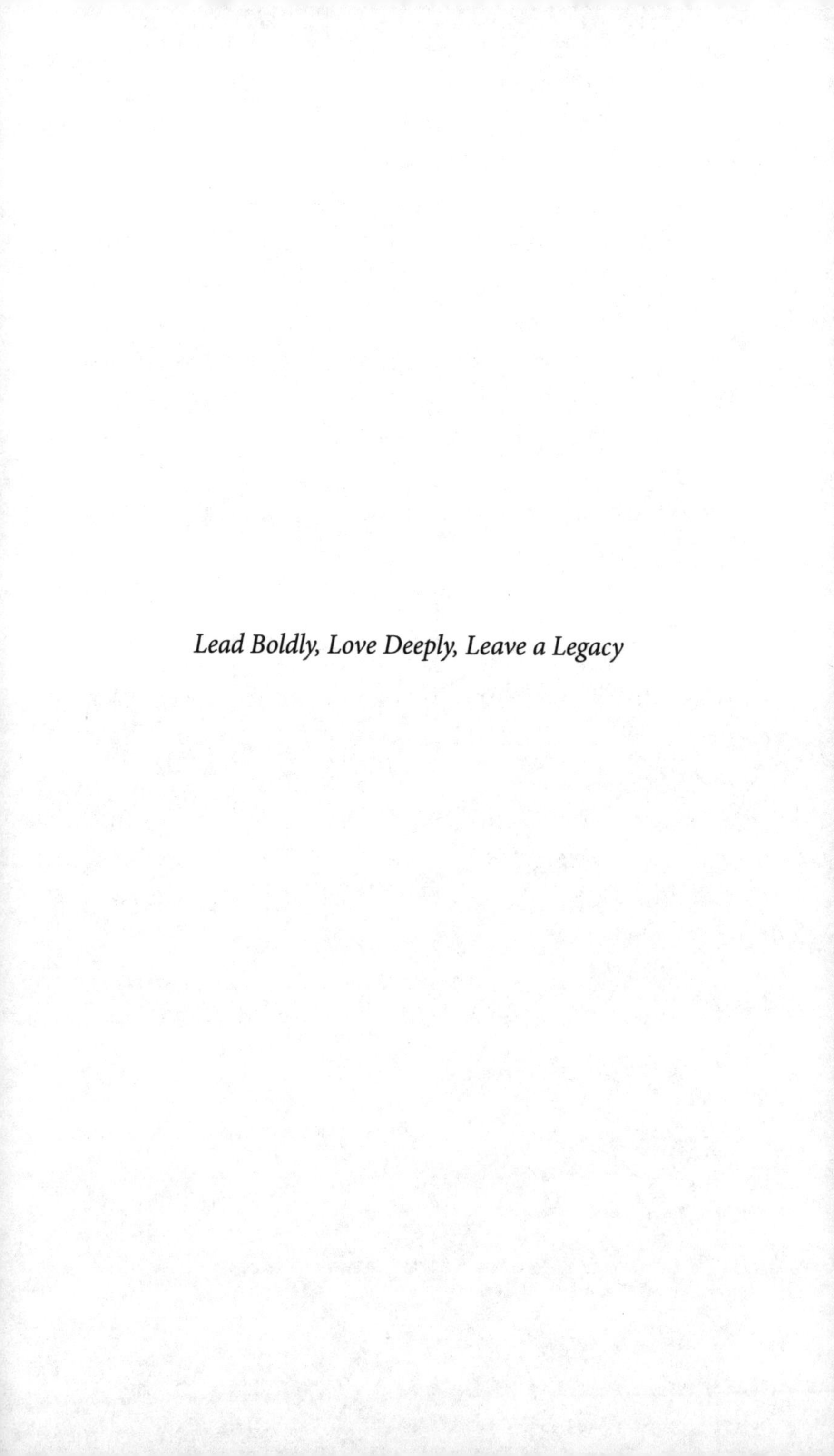

Lead Boldly, Love Deeply, Leave a Legacy

CONTENTS

Introduction

YOU WERE CREATED FOR MORE

You were created for more than you can even imagine.

More than the titles you carry, the roles you fill, or the success you've built. You were created as a daughter of the King—chosen, anointed, and uniquely designed with the full capacity to live a life of love, purpose, passion, and peace according to God's plan.

Before the world called you "CEO," "mother," "wife," "leader," or "friend," Heaven called you beloved. You were handcrafted with intention by the God who doesn't make mistakes. Every detail of your design—your creativity, compassion, resilience, and vision—was woven together for divine purpose.

- You are not just here to build a business. You are here to build a legacy.
- You are not just here to chase success. You are here to create impact.
- You are not just here to serve others. You are here to honor the One who created you.

As a SHE-EO, you are called to rise in both grace and power—to lead with wisdom, to create with purpose, and to love deeply. You are called to influence nations and nurture your family. To run boardrooms and still make room at the table for those you love most. You are called to dream boldly, give generously, and rest peacefully.

Yes, you can do it all—but only when you keep God at the center of it all.

The world will tell you that you must choose between purpose and peace, between success and family, between being powerful and being present. But that's a lie from a world that doesn't understand the balance of a Spirit-led life. You were never meant to choose one over the other—you were designed to live fully in both.

When God created woman, He gave her the ability to carry life—to nurture what is small until it grows, to birth vision into reality, and to bring beauty, love, and order into every space she touches. That same creative power lives in you. It's what makes you a builder, a dreamer, a leader, and a nurturer.

Your family circle matters deeply to God. The laughter around your table, the warmth in your home, the prayers you whisper over your children or loved ones—those are sacred spaces where legacy begins. But so are the visions, the businesses, and the dreams He placed in your heart. They, too, are holy.

You don't have to shrink to fit into someone else's definition of success or womanhood. You don't have to choose between building a home and building an empire. You were designed to thrive in both, led by divine wisdom, sustained by grace, and strengthened by peace that only God can give.

This is your reminder:

You are not too much.

You are not behind.

You are not disqualified.

You are becoming—becoming all God created you to be. And in this journey, He will teach you how to walk in rhythm with His plan. You will learn to lead with confidence and compassion, to rest in His timing, and to build with His strength.

Because when you partner with God, you don't just build a business—you build something eternal.

You are a SHE-EO—a woman who leads with faith, loves deeply, gives generously, and lives purposefully. A woman whose life reflects the truth that you can have success and serenity, impact and intimacy, purpose and peace.

So, take a deep breath.

Let go of the pressure to perform. And lean into the divine truth of who you are.

You were created for more than you can imagine—and with God as your Guide, you will become everything He created you to be.

SECTION ONE

IDENTITY, AWAKENING, AND CALLING

Weeks 1-8

1

ARE YOU A SHE-EO?

AWAKEN, ENCOURAGE, EMPOWER, EQUIP

Arise, shine, for your light has come, and the glory of the Lord rises upon you

(Isaiah 60:1 NIV).

You weren't made to shrink back. You were created to rise, lead, and awaken. As a SHE-EO, God has planted dreams and visions in your heart—not just for your own success, but for the impact you are meant to have on the world.

Being a SHE-EO is more than managing a business or building a brand. It's about building a legacy. Every decision you make, every step of obedience, every act of courage has ripple effects that extend far beyond what you can see.

A SHE-EO:

- Awakens vision—recognizing opportunities and calling forth potential in herself and others.
- Encourages purpose—inspiring others to step into their God-given destiny.
- Empowers action—giving people permission and tools to rise.

- Equips others—providing guidance, mentorship, and resources so others can flourish.

You don't wait for doors—you build them. You don't just dream big—you dream God-sized. Every time you rise, others see that it's possible for them to rise too. Your leadership isn't about position or title—it's about impact. Your faith moves mountains, your obedience opens doors, and your voice gives courage to those around you.

The Kingdom is advancing, and God is calling you to lead the way. Surround yourself with other SHE-EO women who uplift and challenge you, keep building, keep dreaming, and keep rising. Your light has come. Shine boldly.

PRAYER

Lord, thank You for calling me to rise, lead, and influence others for Your glory. Help me to awaken vision, encourage purpose, empower action, and equip others to walk in their God-given calling. May my leadership reflect Your light, and may every decision I make bring honor to You. Surround me with women who challenge me, inspire me, and help me grow. Let my life be a beacon of hope, courage, and faith. Amen.

JOURNAL QUESTIONS

1. What dream or vision has God planted in your heart that is bigger than yourself?
2. How can you intentionally encourage and equip others in your sphere of influence this week?

3. Where have you been holding back in leadership, and how can you rise boldly today?
4. Who are the other SHE-EO women in your life who challenge and inspire you to go higher?
5. How can you measure your leadership impact beyond titles, revenue, or status?

I AM AFFIRMATIONS

I AM a SHE-EO, called to awaken, encourage, empower, and equip.

I AM rising boldly into the God-sized vision He has placed in my heart.

I AM building a legacy that reflects God's glory and love.

I AM a light that inspires others to rise into their calling.

I AM fearless in leadership, courageous in obedience, and steadfast in faith.

I AM surrounded by women who uplift, challenge, and empower me.

I AM creating doors, pathways, and opportunities for others to thrive.

I AM walking in purpose, influence, and Kingdom impact.

I AM a SHE-EO who leads with grace, boldness, and integrity.

I AM advancing the Kingdom through my vision, voice, and actions.

2

INTROVERT BY NATURE, SHE-EO BY TRAINING

For God gave us a spirit not of fear but of power and love and self-control

(2 Timothy 1:7 ESV).

Commit your work to the Lord, and your plans will be established

(Proverbs 16:3 ESV).

Purpose rarely fits neatly into comfort zones. As a SHE-EO, you may naturally prefer quiet corners, solo projects, and reflective moments. Crowds, spotlights, and group settings can feel draining or intimidating.

But leadership, influence, and impact are not reserved for the loudest or most charismatic. They are for the faithful. Introverts are deep thinkers, observers, and reflective creators. You process inwardly, feel deeply, and carry ideas that run far beneath the surface. That depth is your strength.

Sometimes it takes intentional training to stretch beyond natural tendencies—not to become someone else, but to step into the fullness of the calling God has placed inside you. That means:

- Speaking up even when your voice shakes
- Showing up with intention even when you feel invisible
- Sharing your gifts, writing, teaching, or leading—even when it's uncomfortable

Boldness is not born; it's built. Visibility is not a requirement for your introversion to be erased—it's a tool for fulfilling your purpose. Every intentional step outside your comfort zone is strength training for your faith, leadership, and impact.

You don't have to be the loudest in the room. You just have to be faithful to what God has asked you to do. Step by step, you'll learn that you can chase your dreams, build influence, and lead—all while protecting your peace and staying true to yourself.

God doesn't need you to change who you are; He needs you to grow into the calling He has placed in your heart.

PRAYER

God, thank You for wiring me uniquely and giving me depth, reflection, and creativity. Thank You that I am not stuck in comfort but invited to grow and stretch. Help me step into boldness when my heart hesitates, speak when my voice shakes, and lead when I feel invisible. Train me to rise into the SHE-EO You've called me to be. Let my faithfulness and purpose bring glory to You. Amen.

JOURNAL QUESTIONS

1. What have I been avoiding simply because it makes me uncomfortable?
2. Am I mistaking my introversion for a limitation?
3. What gift, idea, or message has God placed in my heart that I need to give voice to?
4. What intentional steps can I take this week to stretch beyond my comfort zone for the sake of my calling?
5. How can I balance visibility and influence while protecting my peace?

I AM AFFIRMATIONS

I AM a SHE-EO called to lead with purpose, depth, and faithfulness.

I AM bold even when my voice shakes.

I AM growing into the visibility my God-given assignment requires.

I AM faithful to step beyond comfort without losing myself.

I AM equipped to influence and impact from my unique perspective.

I AM strong, reflective, and resilient in all seasons.

I AM willing to stretch, grow, and rise into my calling.

I AM a leader who honors God with both my quiet and my boldness.

I AM creating platforms for impact while protecting my peace.

I AM living fully into the SHE-EO God designed me to be.

3

STRENGTH IN THE STILLNESS

Be still and know that I am God…

(Psalm 46:10 NIV).

My grace is sufficient for you, for my power is made perfect in weakness…

(2 Corinthians 12:9 NIV).

There is a sacred stillness that we often forget in the busyness of life—a quiet space where the soul can breathe, far from the noise of demands, distractions, doubts, and worry.

Today, by the water's edge, I found that stillness again. The steady rhythm of the waves seemed to echo a divine reminder: strength doesn't always roar. Sometimes, it whispers.

In the hush of God's presence, strength is renewed. It's found in the gentle voice of the Spirit through His Word, in the quiet comfort of His promises, in the awareness that we don't have to strive to be strong—we can rest in His strength instead.

The ocean preaches its own sermons if we're listening. Each wave declares: He is constant. He is powerful. He is near.

Just as the waves faithfully return to the shore, His grace faithfully returns to us—again and again—refreshing and restoring us in the quiet.

Prayer isn't always loud. Scripture doesn't always shout. Sometimes they whisper truth deep into our spirit: You are mine. You are loved. You are enough because I am enough.

Today, strength came not from striving, but from surrender. Not from answers, but from abiding. In the quiet rhythm of the waves and the steady truth of His Word, I remembered—His strength is made perfect in my weakness.

May you find that same quiet strength today—in prayer, in Scripture, and in the stillness where He waits to meet you.

PRAYER

Heavenly Father, quiet my heart today. In the rush and noise of life, help me to find the stillness where Your presence dwells. Teach me that strength isn't always loud or forceful—sometimes it's gentle, peaceful, and rooted in surrender. When I am weary, remind me that Your grace is enough. When I am restless, draw me back to the rhythm of Your peace. May Your Word speak softly but powerfully to my soul, and may Your presence steady me like the waves meeting the shore. In Jesus' name, amen.

JOURNAL QUESTIONS

1. What areas of my life feel noisy or overwhelming right now?

2. When was the last time I felt truly still in God's presence? What helped me get there?
3. How might God be inviting me to trade striving for surrender in this season?
4. What "waves" of His grace have I seen returning to my life recently?
5. How can I create intentional moments of stillness this week to listen for His voice?

I AM AFFIRMATIONS

I AM grounded in God's peace.
I AM strengthened by stillness.
I AM surrounded by His presence.
I AM anchored in grace, not striving.
I AM learning to rest instead of rushing.
I AM filled with quiet confidence through Christ.
I AM steady, because He is my strength.
I AM enough, because His grace is enough for me.
I AM covered by waves of mercy, again and again.
I AM becoming who God designed me to be—strong, peaceful, and whole.

4

ENCOUNTERING JESUS AT THE WELL

TRANSFORMATION BEYOND REJECTION

When a Samaritan woman came to draw water, Jesus said to her, "Will you give me a drink?" …Jesus answered, "Everyone who drinks this water will be thirsty again, but whoever drinks the water I give them will never thirst. Indeed, the water I give them will become in them a spring of water welling up to eternal life"

(John 4:7-14 NIV).

The woman at the well had a complicated past and faced rejection from her community. She went to the well expecting routine, anonymity, or perhaps shame—but she encountered Jesus.

This encounter changed everything:

- Jesus meets us where we are. He doesn't wait for us to clean up first. He sees the truth of our hearts and loves us there.
- Jesus reveals our truth. He gently exposes the areas in our lives that need healing, restoration, and alignment with God's purpose.

- Jesus transforms us. He refuses to leave us as He finds us. Encountering Him daily allows His love to reshape our identity and mission.
- Jesus equips us to love others. Once transformed, we are empowered to go back to the very places or people who rejected us, not with anger or shame, but with the love of God and a testimony of His grace.

For the SHE-EO, this is a powerful reminder: your past does not define your future, and your encounters with Jesus equip you to influence and bless even those who doubted or rejected you.

PRAYER

Lord, I thank You that You meet me where I am, in all my truth, in all my imperfections. Thank You for revealing the areas of my life that need Your healing and transformation. Help me to embrace Your love daily, allowing it to reshape my heart, my mind, and my purpose. Equip me to return to those who have rejected me, not in bitterness, but with Your love and grace, showing them the power of Your presence. Amen.

JOURNAL QUESTIONS

1. Where in my life am I in need of encountering Jesus daily to reveal my truth and bring transformation?
2. What aspects of my past or experiences of rejection have I carried with me, and how might Jesus be calling me to release them?

3. Who in my life has rejected me or doubted me, and how can I reflect God's love toward them today?
4. How do I experience Jesus' love even in my imperfections or brokenness?
5. What "wells" in my life—places of routine, shame, or discouragement—need a daily encounter with Jesus?

I AM AFFIRMATIONS

I AM a SHE-EO who encounters Jesus daily, allowing Him to reveal truth and transform my heart.

I AM loved and accepted by God exactly where I am, even in my imperfections.

I AM being reshaped by God's love to live fully in my purpose and calling.

I AM empowered to forgive and love those who have rejected or doubted me.

I AM a testimony of God's grace, walking in freedom, restoration, and influence.

I AM courageous in sharing God's love with those who need to see His light through me.

I AM continually refreshed by the Living Water that wells up in me, bringing life, purpose, and blessing.

5

DAILY ENCOUNTERS WITH GOD

THE KEY TO WISDOM, STRENGTH, AND A LIFE OF PURPOSE

If any of you lacks wisdom, you should ask of God, who gives generously to all without finding fault, and it will be given to you

(James 1:5 NIV).

But those who wait on the Lord shall renew their strength; they shall mount up with wings like eagles…

(Isaiah 40:31 NKJV).

…in your presence there is fullness of joy; at your right hand are pleasures forevermore

(Psalm 16:11 ESV).

Each new day brings its own rhythm—a mix of challenges, choices, and opportunities. It's easy to drift into survival mode, doing what needs to be done while our souls quietly long for something deeper. But God offers us more than just enough strength to get by. He offers Himself—wisdom for the decisions we face, strength for the burdens we carry, and purpose that infuses every part of our lives with meaning.

When we intentionally set aside time to encounter God—in prayer, worship, and His Word—we invite Him to align our hearts with His. In that sacred space, He grants wisdom that exceeds human logic, clarity that silences confusion, and strength that sustains us through every season.

But daily encounters with God don't only fill us, they transform us.

- Our families feel the shift as patience replaces frustration.
- Our work becomes more meaningful as integrity and discernment guide our choices.
- Our relationships deepen as we love from a place of peace instead of pressure.

When we meet with Him, He awakens us to purpose—not performance. He calls us to build a life anchored in His truth rather than the world's expectations. This is where real joy and lasting fulfillment are found: in His presence.

Each moment with God becomes a reminder that we are not alone, that our story is unfolding with divine purpose, and that He is equipping us daily to live with clarity, courage, and joy.

PRAYER

Father, thank You for inviting me to meet with You every day. In Your presence, I find wisdom for my decisions, strength for my journey, and joy for my soul. Teach me to slow down and seek You first. Align my heart with Your will and fill me with fresh purpose.

Let every part of my life—my thoughts, my work, my relationships, and my dreams—reflect Your love and truth. May my daily encounters with You shape me into who You have called me to be. In Jesus' name, amen.

JOURNAL QUESTIONS

1. How can I make intentional time with God a consistent part of my daily rhythm?
2. In what areas of my life do I need fresh wisdom from Him today?
3. How have I seen God strengthen me in seasons when I've waited on Him?
4. What might change in my work, relationships, or mindset if I truly prioritized His presence each day?
5. Where do I sense God calling me to live with a deeper purpose rather than just productivity?

I AM AFFIRMATIONS

I AM connected to the Source of wisdom and strength.
I AM guided by divine clarity, not confusion.
I AM strengthened daily through God's presence.
I AM walking in purpose and peace.
I AM aligned with God's will for my life.
I AM filled with joy that comes from His presence.
I AM becoming wiser, stronger, and more grounded in faith every day.
I AM a reflection of God's love and purpose in the world.
I AM not striving—I am surrendered.
I AM living a life of meaning, direction, and divine partnership with God.

6

HONEST PRAYERS AND OUR LISTENING GOD

Every morning, I lay out the pieces of my life on your altar and watch for fire to descend

(Psalm 5:3 MSG).

As a SHE-EO, life often brings seasons when everything feels scattered—tasks, responsibilities, emotions, dreams, and disappointments. Psalm 5:3 gives us such a vivid picture:

Every morning, I lay out the pieces of my life on your altar and watch for fire to descend.

It's not about polished prayers or perfect words. It's about honest prayers—bringing every piece of your life to God: the joy, the stress, the brokenness, and the questions.

David shows us a powerful model: he doesn't pretend to have it all together. He shows up early, raw and real, and he waits expectantly for God's presence and action.

Here's a truth every SHE-EO needs to embrace: when we lay our brokenness before God, He doesn't discard the pieces. Instead, His fire transforms them. Just like a mosaic, the fragments of our struggles, failures, and wounds can become part of a masterpiece when touched by God's presence. The cracks, the scars, and the shattered places don't disappear—they are used to reflect His glory in ways our perfection never could.

Meet God at the altar and wait for His fire to come. And the beauty that emerges is a divine mosaic, showing how He can take what is broken and make it radiant, purposeful, and uniquely His. The waiting isn't wasted; the broken pieces aren't discarded. Every piece contributes to the masterpiece of your life and business, reflecting His glory through your leadership, resilience, and faith.

So, show up. Lay it all down. Bring your joys, struggles, and fears. Then watch for the fire—the Holy Spirit transforming your broken pieces into beauty for God's Kingdom. That's how a SHE-EO leads: not by hiding brokenness, but by allowing God to turn it into a reflection of His glory and purpose.

PRAYER

Father, today, I bring You every piece of my life—the joys, the stress, the uncertainties, and my brokenness. I lay them all on Your altar, trusting that Your fire will touch each piece, transforming it into something beautiful for Your glory. Help me to pray honestly, lead with integrity, and trust fully in Your timing. Even when I don't see the fire yet, I believe that You are at work, shaping my broken pieces into a masterpiece that reflects Your goodness, grace, and glory. Thank You for turning my struggles into strength, my cracks into beauty, and my obedience into impact. In Jesus' name, amen.

JOURNAL QUESTIONS

1. What "broken pieces" of your life or leadership do you need to lay before God today?
2. How can you trust that God is using your struggles and imperfections to create something beautiful?
3. In what areas of your business or personal life have you already seen God turn challenges into growth or opportunity?
4. How does knowing that your broken pieces can become part of a divine mosaic change the way you approach prayer and waiting?
5. What would it look like to intentionally watch for God's "fire" in your life this week?

I AM AFFIRMATIONS

I AM bringing all my life, joy, and brokenness to God's altar.

I AM trusting God to transform my broken pieces into beauty for His glory.

I AM seen, heard, and fully loved even in my imperfection.

I AM a vessel of God's glory, reflecting His masterpiece through my life and leadership.

I AM learning to wait with expectation, knowing God is at work in unseen ways.

I AM strong, resilient, and refined through the process of prayer and obedience.

I AM walking in peace, knowing God's fire can heal, restore, and illuminate my path.

I AM a SHE-EO who leads with faith, integrity, and divine purpose.

I AM confident that God can take my cracks, my struggles, and my waiting season and turn them into beauty.
I AM ready to watch for God's fire and let His glory shine through every piece of my life.

7

THE SECRET PLACE HOLDS IT ALL TOGETHER

Whoever dwells in the shelter of the Most High will rest in the shadow of the Almighty

(Psalm 91:1 NIV).

Intimacy with God is the anchor for your capacity. In a world that celebrates hustle, it's easy to believe that your strength comes from how much you can juggle or how well you can manage your time. But no matter how efficient your systems are, how perfectly your planner is filled out, or how many things you check off the list, if your soul is weary and disconnected, it will all feel empty and shallow.

The truth is, productivity is not the same as peace.

- You can be busy and still feel empty.
- You can accomplish so much and still feel anxious and overwhelmed.
- You can be building your dreams and still feel like you're unraveling.

That's because your true capacity doesn't come from how much you do; it comes from how closely you walk with God.

The secret place—that quiet, unhurried, unseen space of intimacy with Him—is not just a spiritual discipline. It's a lifeline. It's where your clarity returns, your burdens lift, your heart softens, and your soul exhales. It's where your striving gives way to surrender, and your chaos gives way to calm.

When you dwell in His presence first, you don't just "fit Him in," you build *from* Him. You start with peace, and you move with purpose. You become less reactive and more rooted. You stop hustling to hold everything together because you remember, He already is.

Psalm 91 doesn't say, "Whoever visits the shelter...," it says, "*Whoever dwells....*"

This is about making His presence your home, not a weekend escape or an emergency room. And from that place of dwelling, you find rest, wisdom, strength, and resilience—and the grace to carry what He's entrusted to you.

PRAYER

Father, pull me close to You, not just when I'm overwhelmed, but when life is quiet, too. Teach me to make Your presence my home, not my last resort, but my first response. Help me build a life rooted in intimacy with You. Let Your peace lead me, and Your voice center me. I release the pressure to hold everything together, and I choose to rest in the truth that You already do.

JOURNAL QUESTIONS

1. What would shift in my day-to-day life if I treated time with God as essential, not optional?
2. Where can I create even 5-10 minutes of space to be with Him, without an agenda, just presence?

I AM AFFIRMATIONS

I AM rooted in God's presence before I run with purpose.
I AM strengthened not by striving, but by abiding.
I AM not held together by my hustle—I am held together by His hands.
I AM calm in the chaos because I dwell in the secret place.
I AM not behind—I am aligned with Heaven's pace.
I AM connected, grounded, and guided.
I AM covered by His shadow and led by His peace.

8

BUILD WITH HIM, NOT JUST FOR HIM

Unless the Lord builds the house, the builders labor in vain...

(Psalm 127:1 NIV).

Unless the Lord builds a house, the work of the builders is wasted...

(Psalm 127:1 NLT)

Your dreams are sacred when surrendered. When God puts a dream in your heart—a business, a ministry, a family, a mission—it's easy to run full speed ahead, fueled by excitement and vision. You start strong, praying fervently, planning strategically, and pouring your heart into every detail.

But somewhere along the way, the pressure creeps in. Deadlines. Expectations. Comparisons. The need to succeed or prove something. And without even realizing it, you can shift from walking with God to working for Him.

But God is not your supervisor. He's your Source. He doesn't need your performance. He wants your partnership.

That doesn't mean the dream isn't real; it means it's sacred. It was never meant to be built by human effort alone.

And God never asked you to carry it by yourself. Your dreams are gifts, not burdens. They are invitations to collaborate with the Master Builder—to listen for His wisdom, to follow His timing, and to rest when He says rest.

Surrender doesn't mean you stop building. It means you stop striving. It means you come back to the place of intimacy and say, "God, I want Your hand in this. Not just Your approval, Your presence." Because what you build with Him will have eternal impact. And it will be marked by peace, not pressure.

So, take a breath today. Lay the dream back at His feet—not because you're quitting, but because you're inviting Him back into the center.

This isn't about control, it's about *collaboration* with your Creator. And He is far more invested in the outcome than you are, because it was His idea in the first place.

PRAYER

> *Lord, I give You my plans, my business, my family—again and again. Let me not just work* ***for*** *You, but* ***with*** *You. Align my heart with Your will, and let every part of this dream reflect Your presence. I surrender the outcomes and the pressure. Teach me to build with open hands and a yielded heart. I want Your wisdom and guidance, not just my hustle. Thank You, Lord. In Jesus' name, amen.*

JOURNAL QUESTIONS

1. Have I been building with God, or simply asking Him to bless what I've already decided?

2. Where might I need to pause, pray, and surrender control again?

I AM AFFIRMATIONS

I AM a co-builder with God, not a solo builder.
I AM aligned with His pace, not driven by pressure.
I AM surrendered, not striving.
I AM building something sacred, not something stressful.
I AM led by wisdom, not just ambition.
I AM supported by the Master Builder, and I trust His timing and direction.
I AM holding the dream with open hands, and I am not alone in the work.

SECTION TWO

SPIRITUAL FOUNDATIONS AND INNER GROWTH

Weeks 9-16

9

ROOTED AND RESILIENT

CONSISTENT FAITH IN EVERY SEASON

> *...When my heart is overwhelmed, lead me to the rock that is higher than I*
>
> (Psalm 61:2 NKJV).

> *She is clothed with strength and dignity; she can laugh at the days to come*
>
> (Proverbs 31:25 NIV).

As a woman of faith—in business, ministry, or everyday life—you know what it feels like to keep showing up when progress feels slow. You pour your heart into your work, your family, your calling—and sometimes, it feels like your effort disappears into the silence. The waiting stretches longer than expected, and you wonder, *Is any of this really working?*

But God calls you to lift your eyes higher. Psalm 61:2 reminds us that when our hearts are overwhelmed, we can be led to the Rock—Jesus—who stands above the storm. He is steady when everything around us feels uncertain. He is constant when emotions rise and results waver.

Proverbs 31:25 paints a picture of quiet confidence: a woman clothed in strength and dignity, who laughs at the days ahead. That kind of faith doesn't come from perfect circumstances—it's born from a life deeply rooted in God's truth. She can laugh because she trusts.

And here's the truth: *breakthrough is built on consistency.* The harvest doesn't appear overnight. It grows through the hidden seasons—when you keep sowing, keep praying, keep showing up, even when the soil looks dry. God honors consistency. Every act of obedience is a seed, and no seed of faith ever goes unseen.

Even in seasons of drought, your faithfulness is not wasted. God sees your effort, your integrity, your persistence, and your trust. Stay rooted in Him. Keep your roots deep and your faith steady. The shift will come—not just because you waited, but because you remained.

Your consistency in faith is preparing you for a harvest that will last.

PRAYER

Heavenly Father, when I feel weary, delayed, or discouraged, lead me to You—the Rock who is higher than my emotions and stronger than my circumstances. Help me to stay rooted in Your Word, steady in my spirit, and faithful in my work. Remind me that no seed sown in faith is ever wasted. You see it all—every prayer, every act of obedience, every moment of quiet trust. Grow in me resilience, patience, and joy in the waiting. I choose to remain consistent, confident that You are working behind the scenes. In Jesus' name, amen.

JOURNAL QUESTIONS

1. In what area of your life are you being called to remain consistent, even when results seem slow?
2. What does it mean for you to be "rooted" in God's truth right now?
3. How has God strengthened your faith through seasons of waiting or challenge?
4. What "small" act of obedience or faith can you continue today as a seed toward tomorrow's breakthrough?
5. How can you remind yourself daily that God sees and honors your consistency?

I AM AFFIRMATIONS

I AM rooted in God's truth and grounded in His promises.
I AM resilient through every season.
I AM consistent, even when results are unseen.
I AM clothed with strength and dignity.
I AM confident in God's timing and process.
I AM unshaken because my foundation is Christ.
I AM faithful in the little things, and God is multiplying my seed.
I AM becoming stronger through every waiting season.
I AM walking in grace, purpose, and perseverance.
I AM trusting the One who turns my consistency into breakthrough.

10

DON'T WASTE THE WAITING

But those who wait on the Lord shall renew their strength; they shall mount up with wings like eagles, they shall run and not be weary, they shall walk and not faint

(Isaiah 40:31 NKJV).

As a female entrepreneur, waiting seasons can feel like silence. Like nothing is moving. Like your prayers are hanging in the air unanswered. But with God, I'm learning that the waiting is never wasted. It's a divine invitation to grow, prepare, and listen more deeply. Waiting seasons are not punishment—they are preparation.

It's in the waiting that strength is built—not just physical or emotional, but spiritual strength that keeps you steady when life feels uncertain. God uses quiet spaces to shape your character, deepen your faith, and teach you to rely on Him in ways you never could if everything came quickly or easily. But let's be clear—waiting is not the same as idleness. Even when you don't see the outcome yet, keep preparing. Keep planting. Keep showing up.

The unseen harvest is still coming, and your obedience in the unseen is part of what brings it to life. What you build in private becomes the foundation for what God reveals in public. And perhaps the most beautiful truth of all: the waiting teaches you to hear His voice.

When the noise of striving fades, you begin to recognize the whisper of the Holy Spirit. His direction becomes clearer, His presence more personal, and your confidence more secure in Him. Think of David in the pasture, Joseph in the prison, and Jesus in the wilderness. None of them was idle. They were being strengthened, refined, and equipped for the assignment ahead.

So don't waste your waiting. Let it refine you. Let it stretch you. Let it strengthen your faith and sharpen your focus. God is working in the silence, preparing you for a season of visible fruitfulness. Breakthrough doesn't begin the day everything changes—it begins in the quiet days of faithfulness when no one is watching.

The waiting is part of the becoming. Stay faithful, friend.

PRAYER

Father, thank You for reminding me that waiting is not wasted when I'm walking with You.

Help me to see this season not as a delay, but as divine preparation. When I feel restless or discouraged, renew my strength and fix my eyes on You—the Rock who never moves. Teach me to stay consistent in the unseen, to keep sowing seeds of faith, and to trust that You are working even when I can't see it. Refine me, grow me, and prepare me for all You have ahead. In Jesus' name, amen.

JOURNAL QUESTIONS

1. What emotions or thoughts arise when you find yourself in a waiting season?
2. How might God be using this time to strengthen or refine your character?
3. What "seeds" of faith or preparation can you plant right now, even before the breakthrough comes?
4. How has God spoken to you or guided you during times of silence in the past?
5. What would it look like for you to trust the process—and not just the promise—in this season?

I AM AFFIRMATIONS

I AM growing stronger in the waiting.

I AM being refined, not forgotten.

I AM faithful in the unseen because God is faithful to fulfill His promises.

I AM rooted in peace while I prepare for purpose.

I AM listening for God's voice more than I'm longing for results.

I AM equipped for what's coming next.

I AM walking in divine timing, not delay.

I AM steady, surrendered, and strengthened by God's presence.

I AM trusting that what I build in the waiting will bloom in due season.

I AM becoming everything God designed me to be—one faithful step at a time.

11

STRENGTH IN THE STRETCH

The Lord directs the steps of the godly. He delights in every detail of their lives

(Psalm 37:23 NLT).

Grace lives in the tension—not the balance. If you've ever tried to keep all the plates spinning—work, family, relationships, rest, health, ministry, and dreams, you've likely felt the weight of chasing balance. The cultural narrative tells us balance is the goal. That if we could just divide our time perfectly and give equal attention to everything and everyone, we'd finally find peace.

But here's the truth—balance isn't biblical, grace is.

God isn't looking for perfect time management. He's looking for surrendered hearts. He doesn't ask you to split yourself into pieces. He asks you to abide in Him and let Him order your steps.

That means your peace won't come from doing everything equally. It comes from knowing what matters most right now and having the wisdom and freedom to follow His lead. Sometimes, your "yes" will look like launching something new. Other times, it will look like pausing to rest or holding space for your people.

The stretch you feel between roles, between responsibilities, between passion and rest, it's not a sign that you're failing. It's a sign that you're alive, that you're growing, and that you're walking out a life of structural tension with grace.

Think of building muscle. They only grow stronger through stretching. And when you stretch with God—not by force, but by faith—He builds you, He covers you, and He sustains you.

Strength doesn't come from having it all figured out. It comes from waiting on the Lord. From learning to listen. From letting go of what's urgent to make room for what's eternal.

So today, stop trying to get it perfectly balanced and start trusting God in the stretching.

PRAYER

Jesus, I give You the tension I feel, the places where I'm stretched, the roles I'm carrying, and the pressure to get it all right. Teach me to stop chasing balance and start choosing grace. Lead me with clarity. Guide me with peace. Stretch me without snapping me—and let every part of this journey shape me into who You created me to be.

JOURNAL QUESTIONS

1. Where do I feel most stretched right now—emotionally, spiritually, or practically?
2. Can I sense God's grace meeting me there?

3. What might it look like to release the need for balance and receive divine guidance instead?

I AM AFFIRMATIONS

I AM growing in the stretch, not breaking.
I AM led by grace, not driven by guilt.
I AM strengthened as I wait on the Lord.
I AM not called to balance everything. I am called to follow God's voice.
I AM being stretched for greater capacity, not crushed by expectation.
I AM exactly where I need to be when I'm walking with Him.
I AM held, led, and empowered—even in the tension.

12

PEACE OVER PANIC

Do not be anxious about anything, but in every situation, by prayer and petition, with thanksgiving, present your requests to God. And the peace of God, which transcends all understanding, will guard your hearts and your minds in Christ Jesus
(Philippians 4:6-7 NIV).

Enter with the password: "Thank you!" Make yourselves at home, talking praise. Thank him. Worship him
(Psalm 100:4 MSG).

When life throws curveballs, choose trust over turmoil. There will always be moments that test your peace—not just the big, life-altering events, but the everyday inconveniences, delays, and unexpected hiccups that stretch your emotional intelligence and reveal what's really going on inside.

For me, it happened on a ministry trip. I had just landed in Oregon to speak at a women's conference, only to find that my luggage had taken a vacation of its own—and decided to stay in Phoenix.

I had a choice to make: panic and spiral or pivot and trust. I chose trust.

No makeup, no clothes for the service, no hair tools, no toothbrush. But thankfully, I had my sermon notes in my carry-on. (Always carry on your messages, friend!)

Instead of falling apart, I laughed, headed to Target, and grabbed the only outfit in my size—a pair of dress pants, a simple tank, and whatever hair and makeup products I could find. It wasn't glamorous, but it was enough. And God? He moved powerfully anyway.

We saw women encounter God, chains break, hope rise, and lives restored. The enemy wanted to distract me, but peace kept me anchored.

The lesson? If we lose our peace every time plans shift or comfort is compromised, we may be trusting our circumstances more than we trust God.

Peace isn't the absence of chaos—it's the presence of God in the middle of it. And often, how we show up in inconvenience reveals whether we're building on convenience or conviction.

Reminder: You can't control your flight path, your lost luggage, or your unpredictable schedule—but you can control your response.

Emotional maturity doesn't mean everything goes smoothly—it means you stay steady when it doesn't. You weren't called to perfection. You were called to presence. You were called to show up, whether in heels or flats, glam or Target clearance, fully anchored in God's peace.

PRAYER

Father, thank You for the reminder that peace is not found in everything going right—it's found in walking closely with You. Help me to see unexpected moments as opportunities to grow, not fall apart. When frustration rises, anchor me in gratitude. When plans change, help me lean on Your presence. May I never allow inconvenience to drown out the voice of the Holy Spirit. Give me discernment to see the enemy's distractions—and the strength to rise above them. I declare that joy and peace are my portion—and I will carry them into every room, every meeting, and every ministry moment. In Jesus' name, amen.

JOURNAL QUESTIONS

1. When was the last time you let frustration rob you of joy or peace?
2. What area of your life feels out of control right now?
3. How can you actively choose trust over panic today?

I AM AFFIRMATIONS

I AM emotionally grounded and spiritually led.
I AM not ruled by circumstance—I am anchored in Christ.
I AM full of peace, full of purpose, and full of joy.
I AM going to respond with wisdom, not worry.
I AM choosing gratitude over grumbling.
I AM going to carry the presence of God—and that's always more than enough.

13

SEASONS CHANGE, BUT STAY CONSISTENT

That person is like a tree planted by streams of water, which yields its fruit in season and whose leaf does not wither—whatever they do prospers

(Psalm 1:3 NIV).

Seasons change, but every season carries a purpose. Each one shapes your character, strengthens your faith, and prepares you for what's ahead.

- Spring reminds you to embrace renewal and new beginnings.
- Summer brings fruitfulness and joy; a time to flourish and give thanks.
- Autumn calls you to let go and find beauty in transition.
- Winter invites you to rest and trust God's unseen work.

Through it all, consistency matters. Remaining steadfast in your faith through every season allows your roots to grow deeper in God. Your circumstances may shift, but your devotion should not.

The changing of the seasons doesn't mean quitting or giving up. It means preparing and growing through each stage—learning, adjusting, and becoming stronger. Growth doesn't come from avoiding hard seasons but from enduring them faithfully. When you stay rooted, God uses every change to build a life of impact that can weather it all.

And remember, how you exit one season determines how you enter the next. If you leave a season carrying bitterness or fear, it can weigh you down. But if you leave with gratitude, wisdom, and peace, you'll step into the next one ready to flourish. Be careful what you carry forward; only bring what builds, nourishes, and honors God. When your faith remains anchored, you will bear fruit in all seasons, just like the tree in Psalm 1.

PRAYER

Father, thank You for being constant when everything around me changes. Help me to stay rooted in You—consistent in faith, strong in purpose, and steady in love. Teach me not to quit when seasons shift, but to prepare, grow, and trust that You're using every change to build a life that glorifies You. May I learn from each season, carry forward only what brings life, and bear fruit that lasts. Amen.

JOURNAL QUESTIONS

1. What lessons is God teaching you in this current season?
2. Is there anything you need to release before entering the next one?
3. How can you stay consistent in faith and purpose when circumstances change?

4. What practical steps can you take to grow through, rather than give up in, this season?

I AM AFFIRMATIONS

I AM rooted, resilient, and consistent in every season.
I AM not quitting when things change—I grow, adapt, and bear fruit through it all.
I AM grounded in God's purpose, and my life is built to weather every season with grace and strength.

14

GRATEFUL IN EVERY SEASON

THE KEY TO GOD'S PRESENCE AND BRIDGE TO WHAT'S NEXT

Rejoice always, pray continually, give thanks in all circumstances; for this is God's will for you in Christ Jesus

(1 Thessalonians 5:16-18 NIV).

If any of you lacks wisdom, you should ask God, who gives generously to all without finding fault, and it will be given to you

(James 1:5 NIV).

You will keep in perfect peace those whose minds are steadfast, because they trust in you

(Isaiah 26:3 NIV).

Enter his gates with thanksgiving and his courts with praise; give thanks to him and praise his name

(Psalm 100:4 NIV).

Life is a journey of shifting seasons—joy and sorrow, clarity and uncertainty, mountaintops and valleys. Yet no matter what we walk through, God gives us two spiritual anchors that steady the soul: praise and gratitude.

Praise is not reserved for the days when everything is going right. We praise God because He is good, He is faithful, and He never changes. Praise lifts our eyes off the problem and places them on the Father who holds our lives in His hands. It becomes, as I often say, a "nerve pill" for the soul—calming anxiety, quieting fear, and ushering in God's peace.

Gratitude works alongside praise as a powerful posture of trust. The Bible doesn't tell us to give thanks *for* all circumstances, but *in all circumstances.* Thanksgiving shifts our focus from what we lack to who God is. It becomes the key to entering His presence—our "password" to His courts, as Psalm 100:4 says.

When we choose to praise and thank God in every season, something shifts in our hearts. Worry loses its grip. Peace fills the spaces where fear once lived. Gratitude realigns us with God's heart, and praise reminds us of His power. And as our hearts become settled, something else happens: God gives wisdom for the journey. Wisdom to make decisions, to see clearly, and to walk with grace even when the way forward isn't obvious. Praise and gratitude open our spirits to receive His guidance.

How we exit one season determines how we enter the next. Leaving a season with bitterness or frustration can carry residue into the new. But exiting with praise and thanksgiving prepares our hearts for God's next move. It becomes the bridge to what's ahead.

Through praise, we gain strength.

Through gratitude, we gain perspective.

Through trust, we receive peace.

Through it all, God gives wisdom for every step.

Today, let your praise rise louder than your problems, and let gratitude become your daily rhythm. These practices don't just change how you feel—they change how you walk, how you think, and how you enter every season with grace, clarity, and unwavering peace.

PRAYER

Father, thank You for being my constant in every season of life. Even when I feel weary, anxious, or uncertain, You remain faithful. Teach me to praise You not only in the good moments but also in the difficult ones. Let my gratitude draw me into Your presence, and let my praise settle my spirit and silence fear. Fill my mind with wisdom, my heart with peace, and my life with steady trust in Your plan. Help me exit this season with thanksgiving and enter the next with expectation. I trust You to guide me, strengthen me, and walk with me every step of the journey. In Jesus' name, amen.

JOURNAL QUESTIONS

1. What is one thing I can praise God for today, even in a challenging circumstance?
2. What can I honestly thank God for in this season, no matter how it feels?
3. How has praise or gratitude helped calm my heart in stressful or fearful times?
4. In what area of my life am I currently seeking God's wisdom and direction?
5. Am I preparing for the next season with a posture of gratitude, or am I holding frustration or fear?
6. What practical steps can I take to practice daily praise and enter the next season with a heart ready to receive?

7. What would it look like to walk in peace instead of worry this week?

I AM AFFIRMATIONS

I AM choosing praise over pressure.

I AM grateful in every season, trusting God's plan for my life.

I AM grounded in God's peace, no matter what I face.

I AM filled with wisdom from the Lord to walk with clarity and grace.

I AM calm, steady, and strengthened by His presence.

I AM releasing frustration, fear, and bitterness to walk freely in His grace.

I AM aligned with God's timing and ready to receive His blessings.

I AM anchored in faith, not swayed by circumstance.

I AM walking with joy and peace that the world cannot take away.

I AM becoming wiser through every step of this journey.

I AM stepping into God's presence with thanksgiving and praise.

I AM trusting God's plan, praising Him in the process, and walking in His perfect peace.

15

DIVINE FLOW

OPERATING IN GRACE, NOT GRIND

Building a business and life led by the Spirit, not by stress.

Take my yoke upon you and learn from me, for I am gentle and humble in heart, and you will find rest for your souls

(Matthew 11:29 NIV).

It is useless for you to work so hard from early morning until late at night, anxiously working for food to eat; for God gives rest to his loved ones

(Psalm 127:2 NLT).

There's a fine line between diligence and striving.

As a SHE-EO—a woman balancing leadership, business, family, and calling—it's easy to blur that line. You want to build well. You want to honor God. You want to provide, grow, and serve. But somewhere between the deadlines, decisions, and demands, you can drift from divine flow into draining grind.

God never called you to build from burnout. He called you to build from being.

Jesus didn't rush. He didn't operate from pressure or panic. He moved with clarity, grace, and divine timing. Every miracle He performed, every conversation He had, flowed from alignment with the Father—not anxiety about the outcome.

That's divine flow.

It's the posture that says, "God, You lead. I'll follow." "Your timing is perfect, even when I feel behind." "I refuse to trade peace for productivity."

Divine flow doesn't mean you stop working—it means you stop forcing. It means you learn the rhythm of grace—doing what God asks, how He asks, when He asks. When you operate in divine flow, your creativity returns. Your clarity sharpens. Your confidence rises—not from striving harder, but from resting deeper. You begin to realize that peace is not passive—it's powerful. And it's not just a feeling, it's a flow.

God is inviting you to build your business, lead your family, and steward your dreams from this sacred rhythm—where your work is worship, and your rest is trust.

So today, pause. Breathe. Re-align. Let the Holy Spirit reset your pace. Because grace will take you where grind never could.

PRAYER

Lord, thank You for the reminder that I am not built to grind—I am graced to grow. Help me to release the pressure to perform and step into Your divine flow. Teach me how to work from a place of rest and trust. Align my heart with Your rhythm, my hands with

Your purpose, and my mind with Your peace. Let everything I build be guided by Your Spirit, not driven by stress. In Jesus' name, amen.

JOURNAL QUESTIONS

1. Where in my life or business do I feel like I'm striving instead of flowing?
2. What would it look like to build from rest instead of rushing?
3. How can I invite the Holy Spirit into my daily work rhythms and decisions?
4. What boundaries or habits do I need to establish to protect my peace?

I AM AFFIRMATIONS

I AM moving in divine flow, not human striving.

I AM aligned with Heaven's rhythm for my business and my life.

I AM led by grace, not grind.

I AM peaceful, purposeful, and positioned for overflow.

I AM building with ease, excellence, and endurance through the Spirit of God.

16

STEADY IN THE CHAOS

Deep calls to deep in the roar of your waterfalls; all your waves and breakers have swept over me

(Psalm 42:7 NIV).

Sometimes the world feels loud, chaotic, and unsettled. Hearts are anxious. News changes by the hour. Our sense of peace can be easily swept away.

But pause for a moment and observe the ocean. The waves move in rhythm—constant, unchanging. Not even the chaos of the world can disrupt their steady rise and fall. It's a quiet, powerful reminder that God's presence remains unmoved and unwavering.

Psalm 42:7 speaks into this very place of unrest: "*Deep calls to deep in the roar of your waterfalls....*" Even in the roar of the waves, our worries, or the chaos around us, God is calling us deeper. His Spirit speaks to the depths of our souls, offering not escape, but alignment—a steadying rhythm that anchors us when everything else shakes.

The rhythmic movement of the ocean is an invitation:

- Slow down.
- Come closer.

- Breathe.
- Let God set the pace.

Here's the powerful truth: just as the ocean waves cannot be stopped, neither can the plans and purposes of God in your life when you are aligned with Him. When you walk in rhythm with Him—aligning your heart, steps, and focus with His will—nothing in this chaotic world can cancel what God has called you to do.

His purpose is not shaken by headlines. His calling is not revoked by storms. You were created on purpose, for purpose, and God is faithful to finish what He started in you.

And it's not just about individuals—it's about a generation. A generation that rises and aligns with God in the middle of chaos will become a force the world cannot ignore. Just like crashing waves shape the shore, this generation will awaken the earth to God's power—moving in unity, divine rhythm, and unstoppable momentum.

PRAYER

Father, when the world feels chaotic, and my heart feels unsteady, draw me into Your rhythm. Let Your Spirit calm the storm inside me. Help me trust that even when everything feels uncertain, You are not shaken. Steady me with Your presence and align me with Your purpose. Raise up a generation that moves in rhythm with You—bold, unshakable, and awakened by Your Spirit. Let us be like crashing waves—constant, powerful, and impossible to ignore. In Jesus' name, amen.

JOURNAL QUESTIONS

1. Where in my life do I feel most unsettled or anxious right now?
2. How can I invite God's rhythm into these areas today?
3. Am I reacting to chaos or intentionally aligning with God's presence?
4. What steps can I take to be a steady influence in my family, workplace, or community?
5. How can I participate in shaping a generation that moves in God's rhythm?

I AM AFFIRMATIONS

I AM steady in the chaos because God is my anchor.
I AM aligned with His rhythm, not swayed by the storms around me.
I AM unshaken because His presence is constant in my life.
I AM a wave of God's purpose, moving with power and unity.
I AM bold, faithful, and unstoppable in the plans He has for me.
I AM calm in uncertainty because God orders my steps.
I AM part of a generation rising in alignment with Heaven.

SECTION THREE

VISION, DREAMS, AND PREPARATION

Weeks 17-24

17

DREAM NAPKINS AND WHITEBOARD VISIONS

WRITING THE VISION, BUILDING THE LEGACY

> *...Write the vision and make it plain on tablets, that he may run who reads it*
>
> (Habakkuk 2:2 NKJV).

Every great move of God starts with a whisper—a dream, a spark, a glimpse of what could be. For the faith-filled SHE-EO, those dreams often come while sipping coffee, sitting at a red light, or waking up at 3 a.m. with an idea that refuses to let go.

But here's the truth: a dream left unspoken eventually fades, and a dream left unwritten easily drifts away.

That's why God told Habakkuk to *write the vision and make it plain*. There's power in putting pen to paper—or, in modern terms, marker to whiteboard. Writing your vision is not just good business practice; it's an act of faith. It says, "Lord, I believe You've placed this in me, and I'm partnering with You to bring it to life."

So go ahead—grab a napkin, a journal, or that big whiteboard in your office. Write the dream. Sketch the plan. Create a timeline. Dream with discipline.

This isn't about striving, it's about stewardship. When you write out your dreams and build a strategy, you're not trying to control God's timing—you're showing Him you're ready. Your napkin notes become blueprints. Your whiteboard becomes a war room. Your timeline becomes a testimony in progress.

And years from now, when you look back at those scribbles—the prayers, the sketches, the messy drafts—you'll see how God took what started as ink on a napkin and turned it into a living legacy.

So, dream boldly. Write it down. Plan with purpose. Then hand it back to God and watch Him do more than you could have ever imagined. Because what starts as your vision becomes *His victory story.*

PRAYER

Father, thank You for planting dreams in my heart that are meant to bless others and honor You. Today, I choose to write the vision and make it plain. Give me divine strategy, creative insight, and the courage to take small steps toward big faith. Let my planning be led by Your Spirit, and may every dream align with Your purpose for my life, my family, and my business. Turn my scribbles into blueprints for legacy. In Jesus' name, amen.

JOURNAL QUESTIONS

1. What dream or idea has been stirring in your heart that you haven't written down yet?
2. What's one practical step you can take this week to move that dream from vision to plan?
3. How can you include your family in building a legacy of faith and purpose?
4. Where do you need to surrender control and trust God with the timing?

I AM AFFIRMATIONS

I AM a visionary woman, led by the Spirit and guided by purpose.

I AM disciplined in my dreaming and intentional in my planning.

I AM building not just a business, but a legacy that honors God.

I AM co-creating with Heaven, one idea, one plan, and one prayer at a time.

I AM trusting God's timing, knowing He turns my written vision into a living reality.

18

DIVINE DOWNLOADS

LEANING INTO GOD FOR CREATIVE STRATEGY

Seeing beyond now to build what Heaven is revealing next.

This is what the Lord says—your Redeemer, the Holy One of Israel: "I am the Lord your God, who teaches you what is best for you, who directs you in the way you should go"

(Isaiah 48:17 NIV).

I, wisdom, dwell with prudence, and find out knowledge of witty inventions

(Proverbs 8:12 KJV).

Then the Lord said to me, "Write my answer plainly on tablets.... This vision is for a future time. It describes the end, and it will be fulfilled. If it seems slow in coming, wait patiently, for it will surely take place..."

(Habakkuk 2:2-3 NLT).

Every faith-filled SHE-EO carries a spark of divine creativity, because you were made in the image of the Creator Himself. The same God who spoke galaxies into existence still breathes fresh ideas, blueprints, and innovations into His daughters today.

But here's the truth: the greatest business ideas aren't born from striving, they're downloaded in stillness.

When you *lean into God*—not just as your Savior but as your Strategist—you begin to access heavenly insight that the world can't replicate. Ideas that bless people, create impact, and open streams of income that reflect God's abundance, not your anxiety.

Too often, we pray for provision without realizing that God's provision often comes *through* a God-inspired idea. He doesn't just drop money from Heaven; He drops strategy. He doesn't just hand out success; He releases vision.

And the visionary SHE-EO doesn't just see what's happening *now*—she sees *next*. She leans in and listens. She builds with God's blueprint, not the world's model. While others are scrambling to react to trends, she's receiving revelations that set the trends. Because she knows that when Heaven downloads it, it carries an anointing for multiplication.

Ask Joseph, who built an economic strategy that saved nations.

Ask the Proverbs 31 woman who diversified her income with creativity and wisdom.

Ask Noah who built what had never been seen before, simply because he listened.

God is still giving "witty inventions," creative concepts, and strategic blueprints to His daughters who will make space to hear.

So, pause the noise. Open your journal. Clear the mental clutter. Ask the Holy Spirit: "What do You want to build with me?"

Your next income stream, product, or business expansion might not come from hustle—but from a holy download.

PRAYER

Father, thank You for being the ultimate Creator and the Source of all wisdom. I surrender my business, my ideas, and my imagination to You. Teach me to lean into Your Spirit for divine downloads and futuristic vision. Reveal the strategies, products, and partnerships that align with Heaven's plan for my life. Give me the courage to move beyond what's comfortable and build what You are breathing on. May every idea bring glory to Your name and create legacy, impact, and increase—not just for me, but for the generations to come. In Jesus' name, amen.

JOURNAL QUESTIONS

1. Am I creating enough stillness in my life to *hear* creative strategy from God?
2. What new idea, product, or service has God been whispering to my spirit that I've been afraid to pursue?
3. How can I build systems that allow multiple streams of income without burning out my purpose?
4. What am I doing today that will prepare me for the future vision God is revealing?

I AM AFFIRMATIONS

I AM a SHE-EO who creates with Heaven's blueprint.

I AM aligned with divine strategy and Holy Spirit wisdom.

I AM open to God-breathed ideas that create impact and income.

I AM futuristic in faith, not limited by the present.

I AM led by peace, not pressure.

I AM a vessel for God's creativity—everything I build carries His anointing.

I AM walking boldly into the future God is revealing to me—full of vision, purpose, and abundance.

19

ACTIVATE THE DOWNLOAD

TURNING VISION INTO STRATEGY

Revelation is only powerful when it's followed by action.

...Faith by itself, if it is not accompanied by action, is dead

(James 2:17 NIV).

Commit your actions to the Lord, and your plans will succeed

(Proverbs 16:3 NLT).

...Write the vision and engrave it plainly on [clay] tablets so that the one who reads it will run

(Habakkuk 2:2 AMP).

A true SHE-EO doesn't just *hear* from God, she *acts* on what she hears. Divine revelation is powerful, but without activation, it remains potential instead of purpose.

When God downloads an idea, it's a sacred trust—a seed of Heaven placed in your spirit. But seeds only grow when they're *planted* and *nurtured.* That means taking the divine inspiration you've received and turning it into intentional action: strategy, structure, and stewardship.

Sometimes the gap between where you are and what God has shown you feels wide. But remember this: God gives vision in advance because He intends to walk with you in the building process. He's not asking you to have it all figured out. He's asking you to start.

Faith builds. Fear freezes. And every time you choose obedience over overthinking, you shorten the distance between revelation and reality.

1. Write the vision.
2. Pray over it.
3. Plan with excellence.
4. And then move, even if your voice shakes, even if the steps are small.

The SHE-EO who walks with God doesn't just dream about multiple streams of income, expansion, or legacy; she *builds* them through Spirit-led strategy. She learns to partner her faith with focus.

Ask God to reveal the *next right step*—not all of them, just the next one. Then move. He'll meet you in motion. Because Heaven's ideas were never meant to stay in journals—they were meant to transform the marketplace.

PRAYER

Father, thank You for trusting me with divine ideas and vision. I don't want to just dream with You—I want to build with You. Help me to move beyond inspiration into intentional action. Give me clarity, strategy, and courage to take the next step. Surround me with wise counsel and divine timing. Let everything I create carry Your excellence and anointing. May my work produce fruit that lasts and glorifies You. In Jesus' name, amen.

JOURNAL QUESTIONS

1. What divine idea or vision have I received that I haven't yet acted on?
2. What's one tangible step I can take this week to move that idea forward?
3. Am I inviting God into both my creativity *and* my execution?
4. How can I create systems, accountability, and structure to support the vision God has given me?

I AM AFFIRMATIONS

I AM a woman of action, not just inspiration.
I AM a faith-filled builder who turns vision into reality.
I AM led by divine strategy and empowered by the Holy Spirit.
I AM disciplined, focused, and aligned with God's timing.
I AM a SHE-EO who executes with excellence and builds legacy.
I AM walking in obedience, and Heaven backs my every step.
I AM activating what God has deposited in me—and it will multiply for His glory.

20

DIVINE STRATEGY

GROWING WITH INTENTION

Don't just go through seasons, grow with them.

> *Teach us to number our days, that we may gain a heart of wisdom*
>
> (Psalm 90:12 NIV).

> *Commit to the Lord whatever you do, and He will establish your plans*
>
> (Proverbs 16:3 NIV).

As a SHE-EO, you wear many hats—leader, wife, mother, friend, visionary, daughter of God. Each role demands time, energy, and focus. But without intentional growth—both personally and professionally—your days can easily become a cycle of busyness without progress.

There's a difference between *activity* and *advancement.* Between *motion* and *momentum.*

And between working hard and growing wise.

God didn't call you to endless hustle; He called you to strategic growth. Psalm 90:12 reminds us that wisdom begins when we learn to number our days—to see time as sacred, not disposable. Every day is an opportunity to steward what God has entrusted to you: your gifts, your influence, your calling, your business, your family, and your future.

Developing a growth strategy isn't worldly ambition—it's spiritual alignment.

It's asking God, "What do You want to grow in me this season? And what do You want to grow *through* me?"

Self-growth and business growth are not separate—they're connected. You are the vessel through which your vision flows. If you grow, everything connected to you grows.

That's why intentional planning matters:

- Create a *personal growth plan*—books to read, skills to sharpen, mentors to learn from, habits to form.
- Develop a *business strategy*—systems that free you, not enslave you; goals that align with your purpose, not just profit.
- Schedule *rest and reflection*—because revelation often comes in rest, not in a rush.

You can waste months reacting, or you can redeem time by building with purpose. The choice is yours. So today, pause. Reflect. Strategize with God. Ask Him to reveal what's worth your time—and what's just draining it. Because a faith-filled woman with a Spirit-led strategy is unstoppable.

PRAYER

Father, thank You for entrusting me with dreams, influence, and purpose. I don't want to drift through my days—I want to grow through them. Teach me to number my days and to use my time wisely. Show me what to prioritize, what to release, and how to align my plans with Your will. Give me a strategy from Heaven for my growth and my business. I surrender my agenda to You and invite You to lead every step. In Jesus' name, amen.

JOURNAL QUESTIONS

1. Where in my life or business have I been busy but not fruitful?
2. What's one area God is calling me to grow in personally this season?
3. How can I create space in my schedule to seek God's strategy before making big decisions?
4. What systems or habits could I develop to steward my time, gifts, and influence better?

I AM AFFIRMATIONS

I AM a woman of divine strategy, not scattered effort.

I AM growing daily—in wisdom, in purpose, and in excellence.

I AM disciplined, focused, and Spirit-led in my decisions.

I AM a builder of systems that serve my calling, not steal my peace.

I AM redeeming my time, walking in alignment with Heaven's plan

21

BUILD YOUR BRAVE

THE POWER OF YOUR CIRCLE

Who you surround yourself with can shape who you become.

Walk with the wise and become wise, for a companion of fools suffers harm

(Proverbs 13:20 NIV).

Let us think of ways to motivate one another to acts of love and good works. And let us not neglect our meeting together...but encourage one another...

(Hebrews 10:24-25 NLT).

One of the greatest life—and business—upgrades you can give yourself? Surround yourself with the right circle of women.

Not just women who look successful on the outside—but women who carry the presence of God, who love deeply, lead boldly, and grow relentlessly. Women who don't just talk faith—they walk it out. Women who understand that leadership, influence, and impact are fueled by purpose and prayer.

We were never created to grow in isolation. God designed us to thrive in community—especially a community that stretches us, sharpens us, and speaks life over us.

Imagine a room filled with women who:

- Cheer for each other genuinely—without competing.
- Pray, not gossip.
- Celebrate wins—even if they haven't seen their own yet.
- Create atmospheres where the Holy Spirit is welcome.
- Know their worth and encourage you to rise into yours.
- Take big leaps of faith—even when they're scared.

These are not perfect women. But they are purposeful women—the kind who have done the heart work and the hard work, and who invite you to do the same.

If you don't have a circle like this yet, don't be discouraged—but don't stay stuck either. Sometimes, finding your tribe means getting into new rooms, taking risks, and being vulnerable with women who are walking the same upward road of leadership and impact. It may feel uncomfortable at first. You may wonder if you belong. But sister—you do.

This kind of community is not about perfection—it's about presence, purpose, and pushing one another toward the fullness of who God created us to be. So today, ask yourself:

- Are the women around me helping me grow as a leader, entrepreneur, and woman of faith—or holding me back?
- Do I need to step into new spaces where iron sharpens iron?

Because the right circle doesn't just support you—it transforms you. And in that transformation, your influence, business, and legacy rise to the next level.

PRAYER

Father, thank You for the gift of godly sisterhood. Help me discern the relationships that are helping me grow and the ones that may be holding me back. Give me the courage to step into new rooms, even when it feels uncomfortable. Surround me with women who love You, love others, and live on purpose. Teach me to be that kind of woman for someone else—one who lifts, encourages, sharpens, and celebrates. Build my brave, Lord—and bring the right circle into my life for this season of leadership, influence, and impact. In Jesus' name, amen.

JOURNAL QUESTIONS

1. Do the women in my current circle call out the best in me—in business, leadership, and faith?
2. Am I surrounding myself with faith-filled, growth-minded, Spirit-led women?
3. Where might God be asking me to step into a new circle—even if it feels scary?
4. Am I also becoming the kind of woman I want to be surrounded by?

I AM AFFIRMATIONS

I AM a SHE-EO who values godly community.

I AM surrounded by women who sharpen, stretch, and support me.

I AM stepping into rooms where faith, leadership, and purpose are ignited.

I AM becoming the kind of woman I want to walk with.

I AM bold enough to grow, brave enough to try, and wise enough to choose the right circle.
I AM going to build my brave—with God and with the tribe He's bringing into my life.

22

THE CIRCLE OF INFLUENCE

The people you empower are the measure of your leadership.

Two are better than one, because they have a good return for their labor: If either of them falls down, one can help the other up...

(Ecclesiastes 4:9-10 NIV).

Love each other with genuine affection, and take delight in honoring each other

(Romans 12:10 NLT).

As a SHE-EO, you understand that success isn't built in isolation—it's birthed in community. The strength of your leadership isn't just seen in what you build, but in who you build up along the way.

In a world that often celebrates competition, God calls His daughters to cultivate collaboration. He reminds us that our influence is meant to *serve*, not to *shine alone*. Kingdom leadership means creating spaces where every woman at the table feels seen, valued, and capable of rising higher.

As a faith-filled entrepreneur, your business is more than a brand; it's a platform for impact. Whether you're leading a team, mentoring emerging leaders, or collaborating with peers, your influence carries the power to multiply vision, not just execute it.

True leadership isn't about being the loudest voice in the room; it's about creating a room where every voice matters. It's about mentoring without ego, celebrating without comparison, and honoring others even when their success comes before yours.

When you intentionally build circles where women thrive—spiritually, personally, and professionally—you model the heart of Christ: servant leadership. Your business flourishes because you've chosen to sow empowerment instead of envy, generosity instead of jealousy, and connection instead of competition.

And here's the truth: when your circle wins, you win. When the women God has placed in your sphere of influence grow, your legacy expands. That's what Kingdom leadership looks like—every woman rising together under the banner of faith, purpose, and love.

PRAYER

Father, thank You for surrounding me with incredible women who are visionaries, dreamers, and builders of purpose. Help me lead like Jesus: with humility, grace, and a heart to serve. Teach me to celebrate others sincerely and to create environments where women can rise and thrive. Remove any spirit of competition or comparison from my heart, and replace it with confidence in Your calling and joy in the success of others. May my leadership reflect Your Kingdom, where collaboration is strength, love is the foundation, and every win glorifies You. In Jesus' name, amen.

JOURNAL QUESTIONS

1. Who in my circle might God be calling me to mentor, encourage, or empower in this season?
2. Am I building a culture in my business that reflects collaboration and Kingdom-minded growth?
3. How can I celebrate the success of others without falling into comparison or insecurity?
4. In what new ways might God be calling me to expand my circle, to bring new voices to the table?

I AM AFFIRMATIONS

I AM a Kingdom-minded SHE-EO who empowers others to rise.

I AM a bridge builder, not a competitor.

I AM creating spaces of belonging, collaboration, and growth.

I AM using my leadership to multiply faith, purpose, and excellence.

I AM surrounded by women who sharpen, celebrate, and support each other.

I AM building a legacy of empowerment, unity, and impact.

23

STOP PLAYING SMALL

FOR THE FEMALE ENTREPRENEUR WHO'S DONE WAITING FOR PERMISSION

...And who knows but that you have come to your royal position for such a time as this?

(Esther 4:14 NIV).

She wraps herself in strength, might, and power in all her works

(Proverbs 31:17 TPT).

There comes a moment in every Kingdom woman's journey when she realizes—she's not here to revive what used to work. She's here to build what's next.

That moment may not come with fireworks or fanfare, but it does come with clarity. Clarity that you've outgrown old strategies. Clarity that some of the things you once called "faithfulness" were really fear in disguise. Clarity that playing small is no longer obedience—it's disobedience dressed up as humility.

You've been faithful in the small—now God is calling you to be bold in the next. This isn't about chasing hustle or numbers. It's about honoring the mission that's been stirring in your spirit for months—maybe even years.

You don't need to go backward. You don't need to keep "tweaking" what God is asking you to release. And you don't need to keep waiting for someone else to validate what He's already confirmed.

This is about aligned action—the kind that flows from intimacy with God, courage in your gut, and clarity in your spirit. You are not here to blend in. You're here to build—with boldness, with excellence, and with Heaven's strategy.

There are people who need your voice. There are clients who are praying for the exact solution God placed in your hands. There is Kingdom impact attached to your obedience. So no, you're not being "extra." You're being obedient. You're being available. You're being who God called you to be—unapologetically.

This is your month to rise. To grow. To serve. To lead. And the only thing standing between you and that next wave of impact is the courage to make your next move.

PRAYER

Father, I release the fear of being too much. I surrender the pressure to play it safe. Give me the clarity to see what You're building through me—and the boldness to take action without apology. Remind me that my voice carries answers, and my obedience carries weight. I don't want to recycle the past—I want to partner with You for what's next. Help me show up with confidence, consistency, and faith—because this mission isn't about me. It's about what You want to release through me. In Jesus' name, amen.

JOURNAL QUESTIONS

1. Where have I been shrinking back out of fear, not wisdom?
2. What have I been "tweaking" that God might be asking me to release boldly?
3. What's one bold, obedient action I can take this week to step toward the next level?

I AM AFFIRMATIONS

I AM not here to repeat the past—I am called to build what's next.

I AM equipped, anointed, and assigned for such a time as this.

I AM not playing small to make others comfortable—I rise in obedience to God.

I AM speaking with clarity. I move with boldness. I lead with purpose.

I AM not waiting for perfect—I move with faith.

I AM done playing it safe. I am here to build with Heaven's strategy.

I AM the woman for this mission—and I'm just getting started.

24

PICK UP A SHOVEL AND DIG

RECLAIM YOUR PROMISED WELLS

Isaac reopened the wells that had been dug in the days of his father Abraham, which the Philistines had stopped up after Abraham died, and he gave them the same names his father had given them

(Genesis 26:18 NIV).

Isaac inherited more than land—he inherited promises and a legacy. But the enemy tried to stop the flow. Wells that had been dug by Abraham for sustenance, blessing, and provision were stopped up by opposition. Isaac faced resistance, yet he persisted, dug again, and reclaimed what was rightfully his.

As a SHE-EO, the wells in your life are symbolic of the blessings, opportunities, and freedom God has promised you. The enemy may try to throw dirt in your wells, causing delays, disputes, or discouragement, but God calls you to dig, reopen, and reclaim.

Let's look at each well Isaac reopened and what it represents:

1. *ESEK* – DISPUTE OR ARGUMENT

- Meaning: "Dispute" or "contention." When Isaac dug this well, the herdsmen of Gerar quarreled with him over it.
- Application: In your life and business, there will be disagreements, conflicts, or challenges over resources, vision, or authority. The enemy wants to discourage you or keep you from progress.
- SHE-EO Insight: Persist in digging. Do not abandon the well because of opposition. God's promises are bigger than any dispute. Conflict is often a sign that you're in the right place, digging for something valuable.

2. *SITNAH* – OPPOSITION

- Meaning: "Hatred" or "opposition." This well faced further obstruction and animosity.
- Application: Opposition will always come when you pursue your destiny or reclaim your God-given blessings. The enemy may stir jealousy, resistance, or systemic barriers to slow your progress.
- SHE-EO Insight: Opposition is not a signal to stop; it's a signal to trust God and dig deeper. Perseverance in the face of *Sitnah* allows you to see breakthroughs and spiritual growth.

3. *REHOBOTH* – ROOM TO FLOURISH

- Meaning: "The Lord has given us room." After digging through disputes and opposition, Isaac finally found a well where there was room to flourish, expand, and thrive.

- Application: Persistence leads to blessing, freedom, and breakthrough. God opens spaces where you can grow without hindrance. Every struggle or opposition is a step toward *Rehoboth*—your place of provision, influence, and legacy.
- SHE-EO Insight: Your *Rehoboth* is waiting on the other side of persistence. The enemy may try to fill your well with dirt, but God provides room to prosper and succeed in alignment with His promises.

LIFE APPLICATION

- The enemy wants to stop your wells: your joy, purpose, family, freedom, or influence.
- Like Isaac, you must pick up the shovel, dig, and persist.
- Every argument, opposition, or obstacle is part of the process to reach your *Rehoboth*—the place where God gives you room to flourish.
- Don't settle for "stopped-up wells." Your legacy, blessings, and purpose are worth the effort.

PRAYER

Father, I thank You for the promises and wells You have placed in my life. I choose today to pick up the shovel, reopen every stopped-up well, and not allow the enemy to steal my joy, purpose, or legacy. Give me strength, courage, and perseverance to dig through disputes and opposition until I reach the room You have provided for me to flourish. May my work bear fruit for generations and honor Your name. In Jesus' name, amen.

JOURNAL QUESTIONS

1. What wells in my life—blessings, opportunities, or purpose—have been stopped up or abandoned that I need to reopen?
2. Where have I faced *Esek* (dispute), *Sitnah* (opposition), or other forms of resistance in pursuing God's promises?
3. How can I persist in digging even when opposition or conflict arises?
4. What does my *Rehoboth* look like—the place of flourishing, freedom, and room to grow?
5. How will reopening these wells impact my family, legacy, and leadership?

I AM AFFIRMATIONS

I AM a SHE-EO who digs with faith, reclaiming every well God has placed in my life.

I AM resilient in the face of disputes *(Esek)* and opposition *(Sitnah).*

I AM persistent, knowing that every challenge brings me closer to my *Rehoboth*—room to flourish.

I AM reclaiming my joy, freedom, purpose, family, and legacy.

I AM bold, courageous, and aligned with God's plan for abundance and influence.

I AM a steward of generational blessings, reopening wells for myself and those who come after me.

I AM victorious in reclaiming all that God has promised me, walking in purpose, authority, and faith.

SECTION FOUR

BUILDING AND LEADERSHIP IN ACTION

Weeks 25-34

25

BUILDING A LIFE YOU CAN LOVE WITH GOD AS THE FOUNDATION

Unless the Lord builds the house, those who build it labor in vain...

(Psalm 127:1 ESV).

As a SHE-EO woman, you carry big dreams—business goals, creative ideas, and a deep desire to make a meaningful impact. But juggling a growing business, nurturing a passionate marriage, and raising a thriving family can feel overwhelming. That's why the foundation matters.

God gently reminds us: Don't build alone. When we partner with Him and align our vision with His purpose, we begin to experience a divine rhythm—where our business thrives, our personal growth deepens, and our home life is strengthened.

The path to purpose is already full of twists and turns—but trying to navigate it in your own strength makes the journey heavier, more confusing, and often exhausting. Without God as your guide, even the most passionate pursuits can feel aimless. His strength brings clarity where there's chaos, and direction where there's doubt.

You don't have to choose between success and family, faith and ambition, calling and contentment. When God is at the center, these things don't compete—they complement.

Ask yourself today:

- Am I inviting God into every area—my business, ministry, marriage, and home?
- Are my goals rooted in His purpose or just my pressure?
- Is my vision fueled by faith or fear?

When God builds with you, He doesn't just bring success—He brings peace, balance, and joy.

PRAYER

Lord, thank You for entrusting me with dreams and responsibilities. Help me to build my business, ministry, home, and life on Your wisdom. Align my goals with Your purpose, and guide me in a rhythm that honors You and blesses my family. Teach me to trust Your timing, rely on Your strength, and walk confidently in the path You've set for me. In Jesus' name, amen.

JOURNAL QUESTIONS

1. Am I building my life on God's foundation or my own strength?
2. In which areas of my business, marriage, or personal life do I need more guidance from God?
3. Are my current goals aligned with God's purpose or driven by pressure and expectation?

4. How can I invite God into my daily decisions and long-term plans?
5. What would it look like for me to thrive instead of just survive in this season?

I AM AFFIRMATIONS

I AM building my life on God's foundation.
I AM trusting His wisdom to guide my decisions.
I AM aligned with God's purpose in my business, home, and family.
I AM thriving, not just surviving, in every area of my life.
I AM walking in divine rhythm, balancing ambition and peace.
I AM equipped to lead with faith, clarity, and joy.
I AM creating a life that reflects God's glory and blessing.
I AM a SHE-EO woman whose foundation is unshakable because God is at the center.

26

SHE BUILT THE ROOM—AND GOD FILLED IT

Let's make a small room on the roof and put in it a bed and a table, a chair and a lamp for him. Then he can stay there whenever he comes to us

(2 Kings 4:10 NIV).

When she reached the man of God at the mountain, she took hold of his feet. ...the man of God said, "Leave her alone! She is in bitter distress, but the Lord has hidden it from me and has not told me why"

(2 Kings 4:27 NIV).

He went in, shut the door on the two of them and prayed to the Lord. ...The boy sneezed seven times and opened his eyes

(2 Kings 4:33,35 NIV).

When you invest in Kingdom purpose, God never forgets. He blesses in the same space you built for Him—even when the enemy tries to steal the promise.

The Shunammite woman was wealthy, respected, and had everything, or so it seemed. But she noticed the man of God passing through her region often. Instead of ignoring the opportunity, she said to her husband: "Let's build him a room."

She didn't wait for a request. She didn't ask for recognition. She simply made room for the presence of God in her everyday life. She used her resources, her discernment, and her hospitality to invest in something eternal.

Kingdom investment does not go unnoticed. Though she never asked for anything, her obedience caught Heaven's attention. Elisha asked, "What can be done for her?" and when he learned she had no son, he prophesied: "About this time next year, you will hold a son in your arms." Her seed of generosity produced a harvest of promise—not in a distant place, but in the very room she had built for God.

Years later, that same promised son fell ill and died, suddenly, tragically, unexpectedly. What did she do? She didn't bury him. She didn't break down. She laid him in the room she built for the prophet—the room of faith, not fear.

Then she declared: "It is well." She went back to the source of the promise—the man of God. And when Elisha returned, he went into the very room she built, prayed, and the child was raised to life.

There is a powerful cycle at work in her story: She built the room → The promise was given in the room → The promise died → She returned to the room in faith → Restoration happened in the same space. She didn't just build a place for a prophet; she built a place where miracles could dwell. Her investment became her inheritance.

For the woman who's been building quietly: You've been giving. Sowing. Serving. You've opened your hands, your heart, and maybe even your home. You've made room—not for applause, but for God. And you wonder: *Does He see me? Will I ever see a breakthrough for what I've given?*

The Shunammite woman says, "Yes, He sees. Yes, He restores. Yes, He blesses where you build."

PRAYER

Father God, thank You for seeing every space we've built for You—every quiet act of faith, every unseen sacrifice. Teach us to make room for Your presence in our daily lives and to invest in what matters eternally. For the promises that feel delayed or lost, we return them to You now. Strengthen our faith to declare, "It is well," trusting that You are the God who restores and brings life where hope once seemed gone. Bless us in the very places we've built for You, and let our lives testify to Your faithfulness. In Jesus' name, amen.

JOURNAL QUESTIONS

1. What "room" have I built in my life (business, time, money, home, etc.) to honor God?
2. Have I ever watched something I was promised feel like it died? How did I respond?
3. How is God inviting me to return to that "room" in faith—believing for restoration?
4. Will you write a declaration like hers: "It is well, because I know the God who breathes life back into what felt lost"?

I AM AFFIRMATIONS

I AM a Kingdom builder—I create space for God's presence in everything I do.

I AM seen by Heaven—no investment of faith is wasted.

I AM a woman of discernment, hospitality, and strength.

I AM a steward of promises and a witness to resurrection.

I AM blessed in the very places I have built for God.

27

POUR WHAT YOU HAVE—GOD WILL DO THE REST

When All You Have Feels Like Nothing

Elisha replied to her, "How can I help you? Tell me, what do you have in your house?"

(2 Kings 4:2 NIV)

"Your servant has nothing there at all," she said, "except a small jar of olive oil"

(2 Kings 4:2 NIV).

This widow was in crisis. Her husband—a man who had served and protected the prophets—was gone. His death left her not just grieving, but in debt, vulnerable, and about to lose her sons to slavery. All she had was a small jar of oil—not enough to solve the problem, not enough to feel safe, and certainly not enough in the eyes of the world.

But it was enough for God.

Elisha didn't offer money or a miracle on demand. Instead, he asked, "What do you have in your house?" God's miracle didn't come from something outside her—it came from what she already had.

Key truths from her story:

1. *Your oil might look small, but it's sacred.* The oil in her house wasn't just cooking oil. It represents the anointing, the gifting, the calling, and the faith she had left. It felt small to her—but not to God. Don't underestimate the value of what's already in your hands. Your wisdom, your faith, your voice, your creativity—it's oil, and it's enough.

2. *Obedience activates the overflow.* Elisha instructed her to borrow empty vessels, go into her house, shut the door, and start pouring. That's all. She had to take a step before seeing results. Obedience isn't always flashy. Sometimes it looks like showing up, closing the door, and doing the quiet work of pouring—trusting that God will fill what you bring.

3. *The miracle was measured by her faith.* She kept pouring until there were no more jars left. Then the oil stopped. The oil didn't run out—the capacity did. God's supply is not the issue. Our preparation and expectations often set the limits. How many jars have you made room for?

4. *God multiplies what you're willing to pour.* She poured in faith. She filled every jar. Then she sold the oil, paid the debt, and had enough left to live on. What started as barely enough became more than enough—because she was willing to trust and pour.

God didn't just rescue her—He empowered her. What you surrender in faith, God will multiply for purpose and provision.

PRAYER

Lord, help me to stop underestimating what You've placed in my hands. Teach me to pour what I have in faith, trusting that You will fill what I prepare. I give You my oil—multiply it for Your glory, for provision, and for legacy. Amen.

JOURNAL QUESTIONS

1. What do I have in my "house" right now—a gift, idea, connection, or skill—that I've overlooked or undervalued?
2. Where is God calling me to pour, even when I feel like I don't have enough?
3. Have I created enough room (vessels) for God to pour into—or have I limited my own capacity?

I AM AFFIRMATIONS

I AM anointed to pour, even when it feels like I'm running out.

I AM filled with supernatural wisdom, strength, and resourcefulness.

I AM creating space for God's provision to overflow.

I AM moving in obedience, and miracles are following.

I AM not empty—I am empowered.

FINAL ENCOURAGEMENT

Dear woman of faith, you may feel like you're down to your last idea, last ounce of strength, last resource. But God says, "Pour what you have." Because what you have is enough when it's surrendered: The oil will flow. The jars will fill. Your house will live. The enemy may try to touch your promise—but he cannot destroy what God intends to restore. Keep building. Keep giving. Keep making space for God. Because the room you create for Him will be the place where He breathes life into you again.

28

BECOMING A MODERN-DAY LYDIA

BUILDING AND HOSTING REVIVAL

> *One of those listening was a woman from the city of Thyatira named Lydia, a dealer in purple cloth. She was a worshiper of God. The Lord opened her heart to respond to Paul's message. When she and the members of her household were baptized, she invited us to her home. "If you consider me a believer in the Lord," she said, "come and stay at my house." And she persuaded us. [Later] …they went to Lydia's house, where they met with the brothers and sisters and encouraged them*
>
> (Acts 16:14-15,40 NIV).

God is raising up women like Lydia—spiritually grounded, business-savvy, and radically available to host His presence and advance His Kingdom. Who was Lydia, and why does she matter today? Lydia was:

- A businesswoman dealing in purple cloth—a luxury item

- A worshiper of God even before she knew Jesus
- A woman of hospitality, boldness, and influence
- The first recorded convert to Christianity in Europe
- The host of one of the first house churches on the continent

Her faith wasn't private. Her business wasn't separate from her calling. Her home and life became the birthplace of revival.

What it means to be a modern-day Lydia:

1. You build with purpose. Lydia didn't just sell purple cloth; she stewarded her success as a way to serve God's purposes. She was prosperous and kingdom-minded, not just profit-driven. Modern Lydias: Build businesses that fund missions, generosity, and ministry; Operate in integrity and excellence; Don't apologize for being successful—they consecrate their success to God.

2. You host the move of God. After Lydia received Christ, her first instinct wasn't to retreat; it was to open her home. She created an atmosphere where: The gospel was preached; People were discipled; Leaders were refreshed; Revival was sustained. Her home became a hub for the Kingdom. Modern Lydias: Host Bible studies, prayer gatherings, business masterminds, and Holy Spirit encounters; Use platforms, social spaces, and influence to welcome God into the home; Are not just spectators of revival—they are hosts of it.

3. You influence beyond the room. Because of Lydia's "yes," the gospel took root in Philippi, and the Philippian church was born. The same church Paul would later write to, saying: *"I thank my God every time I remember you… because of your partnership in the gospel from the first day until now"* (Philippians 1:3,5 NIV). Lydia was that "first day" partner. Modern Lydias: Don't wait to be invited—they initiate; Don't shrink back from spiritual leadership; Know that revival isn't just an event—it's a lifestyle.

PRAYER

> *Lord, make me a woman like Lydia—open-hearted, open-handed, and bold in faith. Let my life and work be a home for Your Spirit, a table for Your people, and a seedbed for revival.*

JOURNAL QUESTIONS

1. What has God entrusted to me that could be a tool for revival (business, home, influence, finances)?
2. Have I been compartmentalizing my faith and work—or is it fully surrendered?
3. How can I build or host space for others to encounter God this season?
4. Am I willing to be the first one to say yes and make room for others to follow?
5. How is my work making space for God's work?
6. What spaces in my life or business can host God's presence?

I AM AFFIRMATIONS

I AM a modern-day Lydia.
I AM a worshiper and a builder.
I AM positioned for Kingdom purpose and Spirit-led impact.
I AM hosting revival in my life, business, and home.

I AM a carrier of breakthrough for my city, my circle, and my generation.

FINAL WORD

Lydia was the start, not the exception. God didn't use Lydia despite her business; He used her through it. She shows us that faith and leadership are not separate. They are integrated, powerful, and world-shifting. So, rise, Lydia. Build with boldness. Open the door.

Set the table. And expect God to move through what you've built—because He will.

29

THE WIDOW OF ZAREPHATH

THE RISK-TAKING PROVIDER

Radical faith in the face of lack.

> *"As surely as the Lord your God lives," she replied, "I don't have any bread—only a handful of flour in a jar and a little olive oil in a jug. I am gathering a few sticks to take home and make a meal for myself and my son, that we may eat it—and die"*
>
> (1 Kings 17:12 NIV).

First Kings 17:7-16 tells of the widow of Zarephath, who is a remarkable example of stepping out in faith when resources are dangerously low:

- She had *almost nothing*, just a handful of flour and a little oil.
- Yet, she chose to obey the prophet Elijah and give away her last meal first.
- She took a risk most wouldn't, and God turned her act of obedience into a continual miracle that sustained her, her son, and the prophet throughout a severe famine.

Lessons for the faith-filled SHE-EO:

1. Faith moves first, provision follows. This widow didn't wait for abundance to serve; she served in scarcity. In business and life, your next breakthrough often starts with a step of faith before the increase.

2. Obedience unlocks God's supernatural provision. Her obedience wasn't just an act of generosity—it was a key to unlocking daily provision from Heaven. When you align your actions with God's word and timing, you position yourself for His miracle supply.

3. God's provision sustains beyond the crisis. The flour and oil didn't just last for one meal — they lasted through the famine. God's provision is often about sustainability, not just quick fixes.

PRAYER

> *Father God, You are the Provider who sees us in every season of leadership—especially when resources feel limited, and the risk feels great. You know the weight we carry as women called to build, lead, and steward what You've placed in our hands. Give us the faith of the widow of Zarephath—to obey when it feels uncomfortable, to give when it feels costly, and to trust You beyond what our numbers, plans, or reserves can guarantee. Teach us to move first in faith, confident that provision follows obedience. Multiply what we surrender. Sustain what You have entrusted to us. And remind us that Your supply is not fragile, seasonal, or uncertain—it is faithful, daily, and more than enough. We lead boldly, trust fully, and rest in You as our Source. In Jesus' name, amen.*

JOURNAL QUESTIONS

1. What "last handful of flour" do I have that God might use to start a miracle?
2. Where am I called to risk obedience instead of playing it safe?
3. How can I trust God's provision beyond immediate needs?
4. What is God asking me to give or do today, even when it feels risky?

I AM AFFIRMATIONS

I AM a risk-taking provider, trusting God to multiply what I surrender.

I AM obedient in scarcity, confident in God's abundant provision.

I AM sustained by God's supernatural supply through every season.

CLOSING ENCOURAGEMENT

When you risk stepping out with what little you have, you invite God's power to work through you. Like the widow of Zarephath, your faith-filled obedience can become the source of ongoing blessing—for you, your family, your business, and your community. So, take the step. Pour out your last. Trust the God who never runs out.

30

KINGDOM BUILDERS

FAITH-FILLED WOMEN IN BUSINESS

She is clothed with strength and dignity; she can laugh at the days to come

(Proverbs 31:25 NIV).

The Lord announces the word, and the women who proclaim it are a mighty throng

(Psalm 68:11 NIV).

Whatever you do, work at it with all your heart, as working for the Lord, not for human masters

(Colossians 3:23 NIV).

God has always used entrepreneurial, bold, and strategic women to advance His Kingdom. You, faith-filled businesswoman, are walking in their legacy—and building on their foundation. God has always used women to build Kingdom impact. You are not an anomaly. You are part of a divine legacy of women who have led businesses, financed ministry, opened their homes, and shifted nations—not from pulpits, but from boardrooms, markets, and everyday obedience.

The Bible is filled with women who were bold in business and faithful in heart. Their stories are not footnotes; they are templates for women like you today.

You have already met a few of the Kingdom businesswomen of the Bible:

1. *Lydia: The CEO and Church Planter* (Acts 16:14-15,40). Lydia was a dealer in purple cloth, a high-end product for the wealthy. She was a woman of influence, wealth, and hospitality. But most of all, she was a worshiper of God.

- She used her business resources to support Paul's ministry.
- Her home became one of the first churches in Europe.
- Her entrepreneurship opened the door for Kingdom expansion.

You are like Lydia when you use your business not just to make a profit but to fund purpose and host God's presence in whatever space you own—be it your office, your platform, or your home.

2. *The Proverbs 31 Woman: The Multi-Stream Maven* (Proverbs 31:10-31). This woman was more than a homemaker; she was a strategic investor, buyer, seller, merchant, and manager.

- She buys real estate (v.16)
- She runs a profitable trade (v.18, 24)
- She manages her staff (v.15)
- She prepares for the future (v.21, 25)
- And she does it all with honor, wisdom, and joy

She proves that God is not intimidated by ambitious women—He celebrates them. You are like her when you build with strategy, steward with excellence, and lead with grace, knowing your work is not worldly, it's worship.

3. *The Widow of Zarephath: The Risk-Taking Provider* (1 Kings 17:7-16). This woman had almost nothing, only a handful of flour and a little oil. Yet God chose her to partner in a miracle that sustained both a prophet and her household during famine.

- She took a step of radical faith with her last resource.
- Her obedience unlocked supernatural provision.

You are like her when you trust God with your business, even when the numbers don't make sense, believing that your little becomes limitless in His hands.

4. *The Shunammite Woman: The Kingdom Investor* (2 Kings 4:8-37). A wealthy woman who noticed the prophet Elisha passing through town and built a room onto her home for him. She didn't ask for anything in return, just honored the presence of God.

- Her hospitality opened the door for prophetic favor.
- Her generosity brought resurrection to her personal life.
- Her story reminds us that spiritual return follows Kingdom investment.

You are like her when you sow into Kingdom work without needing the spotlight, but knowing that God always remembers women who make room for Him.

These women weren't just "helpers" or background characters; they were integral to the move of God in their generation. And so are you. You are not building "just a business," you are building a vehicle for Kingdom influence.

Your company, your creativity, and your capital are all keys in the hand of a woman who says, "God, use me."

You are a:

- Modern-day Lydia building and hosting revival.
- Proverbs 31 woman managing legacy with wisdom.
- Zarephath widow trusting God to multiply.
- Shunammite woman investing into Kingdom movement.

And most of all—you are called.

PRAYER

God, thank You for entrusting me with this business. Let it not just prosper—let it carry Your presence. Make me bold like Lydia, wise like the Proverbs 31 woman, faithful like the widow, and generous like the Shunammite. Use my work for Your glory.

JOURNAL QUESTIONS

1. How is my business positioned to serve God's purposes?
2. Which biblical businesswoman do I most identify with today—and why?
3. Where is God asking me to trust Him more in faith, generosity, or vision?

I AM AFFIRMATIONS

I AM a Kingdom builder in business.
I AM walking in the legacy of women God trusted with vision and influence.

I AM wise, bold, and obedient—led by purpose, not pressure.
I AM positioned for impact, provision, and legacy.
I AM building more than a brand—I'm building for the glory of God.

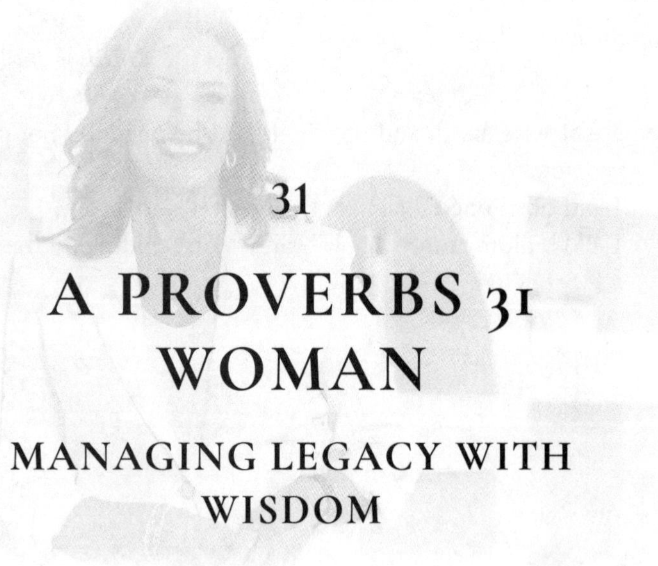

31

A PROVERBS 31 WOMAN

MANAGING LEGACY WITH WISDOM

> *She is clothed with strength and dignity; she can laugh at the days to come. She speaks with wisdom, and faithful instruction is on her tongue. She watches over the affairs of her household and does not eat the bread of idleness. Her children arise and call her blessed; her husband also, and he praises her; …Charm is deceptive, and beauty is fleeting; but a woman who fears the Lord is to be praised. Honor her for all that her hands have done, and let her works bring her praise at the city gate*
>
> (Proverbs 31:25-28, 30-31 NIV).

The Proverbs 31 woman wasn't just virtuous; she was visionary. She built for more than the moment. She managed a legacy with wisdom, strength, and intentionality—and so can you.

What does it mean to manage legacy? Legacy isn't just about wealth or assets. Legacy is about what lives on after you—your values, your impact, your influence, your faith.

The Proverbs 31 woman was not just a homemaker—she was a home-builder, a businesswoman, a mentor, and a faithful steward. Every part of her life was intentional, and because of that, her life echoed beyond her own generation.

Three ways the Proverbs 31 woman managed her legacy with wisdom:

1. She built with the future in mind: "She can laugh at the days to come." She wasn't anxious about the future—she prepared for it. Her wisdom gave her confidence. Her planning gave her peace:

- She invested (v.16)
- She stewarded resources (v.18)
- She clothed her family well (v.21)
- She worked with eager hands (v.13)

She wasn't just surviving; she was strategically building.

2. She used her voice to instruct and influence: "She speaks with wisdom, and faithful instruction is on her tongue." Her influence wasn't just in what she did—it was in what she said. She didn't waste her words. She didn't gossip or complain. She taught, guided, and uplifted with purpose.

3. She was praised because she feared the Lord: "A woman who fears the Lord is to be praised." Her true legacy wasn't just her productivity—it was her devotion to God.

- That's what her children remembered.
- That's what her husband honored.
- That's what the city celebrated.

Her life was built on reverence, not reputation.

PRAYER

Lord, help me build what lasts. Let my words, my work, and my worship leave a legacy that honors You and blesses generations. In Jesus' name, amen.

JOURNAL QUESTIONS

1. What kind of legacy do I want to leave in my family, business, or community?
2. What am I doing today that supports that legacy?
3. What is one area where I need to lead with greater wisdom?
4. Am I making daily decisions that build a future aligned with God's promises?
5. Am I using my words to shape faith, clarity, and wisdom in others—especially the next generation?
6. Am I prioritizing intimacy with God above image, success, or status?

I AM AFFIRMATIONS

I AM a wise woman, building with vision and strength.
I AM managing my time, gifts, and resources with divine purpose.
I AM leaving a legacy of faith, integrity, and love.
I AM not intimidated by the future—I am prepared for it.
I AM a Proverbs 31 woman, praised by Heaven for the life I live today.

FINAL ENCOURAGEMENT

You don't have to be perfect to leave a powerful legacy, just faithful.

Keep showing up. Keep choosing wisdom. Your work may be quiet today, but your impact will speak loudly tomorrow. You are managing more than a moment—you are managing a legacy.

32

DIVINE SYSTEMS

BUILDING WHAT LASTS

But everything should be done in a fitting and orderly way

(1 Corinthians 14:40 NIV).

The wise woman builds her house, but with her own hands the foolish one tears hers down

(Proverbs 14:1 (NIV).

Order is the foundation of overflow. Strategy sets your direction. Systems sustain your destiny.

You can have the most beautiful vision board, the most inspiring dream napkin, and the most powerful God-given idea—but without structure, even divine dreams can crumble under the weight of inconsistency and chaos.

God is the God of order. From the galaxies in motion to the rhythm of day and night, His fingerprints are seen in divine systems. Creation itself is sustained by order, not by accident.

And if you want your business, your ministry, or your home to flourish long-term—you must learn to build like the Father builds: with clarity, structure, and purpose.

Many SHE-EOs live in a state of constant reaction—putting out fires, juggling demands, and running on adrenaline. But systems shift you from reacting to ruling. They create room for peace, creativity, and sustainability.

Systems are not restrictive—they're protective. They free you from becoming overwhelmed so you can focus on what truly matters. They make room for your family, your faith, and your future legacy.

Think about it: The Proverbs 31 woman didn't just survive her schedule—she stewarded it. She planned ahead. She delegated. She operated in wisdom. She built systems that multiplied her impact.

You, too, can do the same. Create systems for your mornings, your meetings, your money, and your mindset. Set rhythms that protect your peace and elevate your productivity. Let structure serve your soul, not suffocate it.

When your life is in divine order, overflow becomes natural. Because God blesses what's prepared to carry the blessing.

PRAYER

Lord, thank You for being the God of order and peace. Teach me how to build with wisdom, structure, and sustainability. Help me create systems that reflect Your excellence and make room for Your blessing. Show me where my time, energy, or resources are leaking—and give me the courage to realign. May my business, my home, and my habits reflect divine order, not worldly chaos. Establish my steps, and help me build what will last for generations. In Jesus' name, amen.

JOURNAL QUESTIONS

1. Where in my life or business do I currently feel the most disorganized or overwhelmed?
2. What systems or structures could I implement to bring peace and productivity into that area?
3. How can I make space in my schedule for both strategy and stillness?
4. What would my daily rhythm look like if I built it around my priorities—not just my pressures?

I AM AFFIRMATIONS

I AM a wise woman who builds with intention and order.

I AM establishing divine systems that create peace and productivity.

I AM a steward of time, talent, and resources—not a slave to busyness.

I AM walking in rhythm with Heaven's blueprint for my life and business.

I AM building what lasts—by God's wisdom, for God's glory.

33

STAY IN YOUR LANE

ESCAPING THE COMPARISON TRAP

> *...Let us run with perseverance the race marked out for us, fixing our eyes on Jesus, the pioneer and perfecter of faith...*
>
> (Hebrews 12:1-2 NIV).

As a SHE-EO, it's easy to look around and see what everyone else is doing—who launched faster, who's scaling bigger, whose brand looks more polished. The temptation to compare can steal your joy, distort your vision, and make you doubt the assignment God placed in your hands.

But God didn't call you to run *their* race. He called you to run *yours.* When you fix your eyes on Jesus—not on competitors, followers, or metrics—you realign your heart with your true Source of success.

You are uniquely equipped for the purpose God has designed for you. The skills, passions, and life experiences you carry aren't random—they are divine tools crafted for your specific calling. There are people only *you* can reach, clients only *you* can serve, and hearts only *your* story can touch. When you try to imitate someone else's path, you step out of alignment with the one-of-a-kind mission Heaven entrusted to you.

The lane God has you in is not too small, too slow, or too late. Every act of obedience, even when unseen, advances His Kingdom in ways you may not yet realize.

Comparison is the thief of contentment, but gratitude restores your focus. Instead of measuring your progress by others, measure it by your faithfulness to what God asked *you* to do.

Stay steady. Stay surrendered. Stay in your lane—because your lane leads to lives only *you* can impact.

PRAYER

Father, thank You for reminding me that You've marked out a unique path for my life and business. Thank You for equipping me with everything I need to fulfill the purpose You've placed within me. Help me to silence the voice of comparison and fix my eyes on You. Teach me to celebrate others while staying faithful to my own calling. Use my business to reach the hearts You've assigned to me and to bring glory to Your name. In Jesus' name. Amen.

JOURNAL QUESTIONS

1. Where have I recently found myself comparing my business or journey to someone else's?
2. How has that comparison affected my peace, confidence, or creativity?
3. What unique gifts, experiences, or perspectives has God given me for my specific assignment?

4. Who might I be called to reach or serve that others cannot?
5. What are three things I'm grateful for in this current season of my business?

I AM AFFIRMATIONS

I AM uniquely equipped and anointed for the assignment God has given me.
I AM running my race with grace, focus, and perseverance.
I AM free from comparison and confident in God's timing and design.
I AM called to reach people only my story and purpose can touch.
I AM building a business that reflects Heaven's excellence, not the world's standards.
I AM content, grateful, and steadfast in my Kingdom purpose.

34

LEADING FROM WITHIN

YOU CAN'T LEAD OTHERS WELL IF YOU'RE NOT LEADING YOURSELF WELL

Above all else, guard your heart, for everything you do flows from it

(Proverbs 4:23 NIV).

Keep a close watch on how you live and on your teaching. Stay true to what is right for the sake of your own salvation and the salvation of those who hear you

(1 Timothy 4:16 NLT).

Remain in me, as I also remain in you. No branch can bear fruit by itself; it must remain in the vine...

(John 15:4 NIV).

Every SHE-EO knows the tension of pouring out. You're leading teams, managing vision, showing up for family, and still trying to stay centered on who you are. But leadership isn't just about *what you do*; it's about *who you are becoming* in the process.

If your inner world is in chaos, it will eventually show up in your outer world. The tone of your leadership flows from the condition of your heart. What's inside you will always duplicate—in your home, your team, and your legacy.

That's why the wise woman doesn't just build businesses, she builds *herself*:

- She tends to her soul before her schedule.
- She leads from humility, not hustle.
- She values integrity over image.
- She strengthens her spirit before she steps on the stage or into the meeting.

Because the truth is, you can't pour from an empty well. You can't lead your team with excellence if you're running on fumes. You can't nurture your marriage or family if you've abandoned your own emotional health. You can't model faith if you're not making space for God to refill you daily.

The world measures leadership by results. Heaven measures it by *alignment*.

A SHE-EO rooted in faith knows that self-leadership is sacred stewardship. When you lead yourself well—physically, mentally, spiritually, and emotionally—you become a living invitation for others to do the same.

So slow down and check your foundations:

- Are you nurturing your body as God's temple—resting, moving, and fueling it with care?
- Are you nourishing your mind with truth, not toxic thoughts?
- Are you staying connected to the Word, letting God replenish what life drains?

- Are you keeping your nurturing spirit alive at home—loving, listening, and being fully present where it matters most?

Before God ever called you to *lead*, He called you to *abide*. And when your leadership flows from intimacy with Him, you'll lead not from exhaustion, but from overflow.

PRAYER

Father, thank You for the influence You've entrusted to me. Teach me to lead myself well so that I can lead others with integrity, humility, and grace. Help me to stay rooted in You—not in performance, but in presence. Renew my mind, restore my body, and realign my heart to Your rhythm. May my leadership flow from a place of wholeness and intimacy with You. Strengthen me to nurture my marriage, my family, and my faith with the same excellence I give my business. Let everything I do reflect Your love and truth from the inside out. In Jesus' name, amen.

JOURNAL QUESTIONS

1. How well am I leading myself right now—spiritually, emotionally, and physically?
2. What areas of my life need recalibration or rest so I can lead from overflow, not depletion?
3. Am I nurturing my home and family with the same intentionality I bring to my business?
4. What daily rhythms can I create to stay connected to God and grounded in His peace?

I AM AFFIRMATIONS

I AM a woman who leads from overflow, not exhaustion.

I AM rooted in humility, integrity, and faith.

I AM nurturing my body, mind, and spirit as sacred stewardship.

I AM a SHE-EO led by the Spirit—grounded, wise, and whole.

I AM leading my family, my business, and myself with grace and balance.

I AM carrying peace and presence into every space I lead.

I AM aligned with God—and from that alignment, I thrive and empower others to do the same.

SECTION FIVE

PERSEVERANCE, RESILIENCE, AND REFINEMENT

Weeks 35-44

35

DON'T LET DELAYED PROMISES KILL THE DREAMER IN YOU

Let us hold unswervingly to the hope we profess, for he who promised is faithful

(Hebrews 10:23 NIV).

There's a deep ache that comes when promises remain delayed or unfulfilled—when the dream God placed in your heart still feels distant, and the waiting stretches on longer than you expected. Over time, it's easy to stop dreaming altogether, to settle for less, or to believe maybe it just wasn't meant to be.

But God didn't plant that dream in you to tease you or break your heart. He planted it with purpose. Though it hasn't happened *yet,* His promise still stands, and His timing is always intentional.

The enemy would love nothing more than to crush the dreamer in you—using the weight of delay to bury your hope. But hope is not dead, and neither are you. If God gave the dream, He will sustain it.

As a SHE-EO woman, your dreams carry Kingdom impact. They are not just ideas—they are seeds of purpose, vision, and influence planted for God's glory. Keep the dreamer in you alive. Keep hoping. Keep creating. Keep trusting. God is still writing your story, and He always finishes what He starts.

Delay is not denial. Waiting is not failure. Your dream is still valid, your vision is still alive, and your promise is still coming—on God's perfect timeline. God is still writing your story, and He finishes what He starts.

PRAYER

Lord, breathe life into the dreamer in me. When the wait is long and the promise feels far away, help me not to lose heart. Remind me that You are faithful to complete what You began. Strengthen me to keep dreaming, keep creating, and keep trusting. I choose to believe again and walk in hope. In Jesus' name. Amen.

JOURNAL QUESTIONS

1. What dream has been delayed in my life, and how have I responded?
2. Am I allowing the delay to kill the dreamer in me or fuel my faith?
3. How can I actively nurture the dream God placed in my heart today?
4. What steps can I take to keep creating and building even while I wait?
5. How does trusting God's timing bring peace and strength in the waiting?

I AM AFFIRMATIONS

I AM a dreamer, and my dreams are alive in God's timing.
I AM patient, knowing that God's promises never fail.
I AM faithful to steward the vision God placed in my heart.
I AM persistent, creative, and resilient in the wait.
I AM filled with hope that grows stronger every day.
I AM guided by God's wisdom to take steps toward my purpose now.
I AM fearless in dreaming boldly for the Kingdom.
I AM standing firm, confident that God will complete what He started.
I AM a SHE-EO woman whose dreams impact generations and glorify God.

36

DON'T LET YOUR HEART FAINT

BREAKTHROUGH IS CLOSER THAN YOU THINK

And let us not grow weary while doing good, for in due season we shall reap if we do not lose heart
(Galatians 6:9 NKJV).

Breakthrough rarely comes to the passive—it comes to the persistent. As a SHE-EO woman, your calling requires faith that refuses to faint, even when the answers seem delayed, and the heavens feel silent.

To faint is more than physical tiredness; it's the spiritual urge to give up. It's the sigh in your prayers, the silence in worship, the weariness in the waiting. Yet Scripture reminds us: *"Do not grow weary...for in due season you shall reap...if you do not lose heart."*

Contending for your breakthrough is about spiritual grit and tenacity. It's Jacob saying, "I will not let You go unless You bless me." It's Elijah sending his servant back seven times to look for rain. It's the woman with the issue of blood pressing through the crowd just to touch the hem of Jesus' garment.

Breakthrough often arrives at the edge of exhaustion. That's where endurance becomes faith's weapon. That's where your groans ascend as incense before God's throne. That's where angels are dispatched, and strongholds begin to crumble.

Delay is not denial. Tears are not wasted. Prayers are never ignored. Heaven sees your persistence, and God responds to those who refuse to quit.

Keep contending. Keep pressing. The harvest is nearer than you think.

PRAYER

Lord, teach me to contend with faith and endurance. Help me to stand firm even when I feel weary and to persist even when answers are delayed. Stir a holy hunger in me to press into You, trusting that breakthrough is coming. Strengthen my heart, steady my hands, and empower me to push forward until Your promises manifest. In Jesus' name, amen.

JOURNAL QUESTIONS

1. What area of my life or business feels delayed right now?
2. Where have I been tempted to grow weary or faint in faith?
3. How can I cultivate persistence and endurance in my prayer life, decisions, or leadership?
4. Which examples of biblical persistence inspire me to keep contending?
5. What one step of faith can I take today to keep moving toward breakthrough?

I AM AFFIRMATIONS

I AM persistent and refuse to grow weary in the pursuit of my God-given calling.

I AM contending in faith, even when the answers seem delayed.

I AM strengthened by God to endure every season of waiting.

I AM a vessel of perseverance, pressing forward with purpose and boldness.

I AM standing firm, knowing that breakthrough is closer than I think.

I AM fearless in prayer, knowing Heaven hears my persistence.

I AM resilient, equipped to overcome every obstacle in my path.

I AM empowered to push, pray, and persist until my harvest comes.

I AM a SHE-EO woman whose faith and endurance shape destiny.

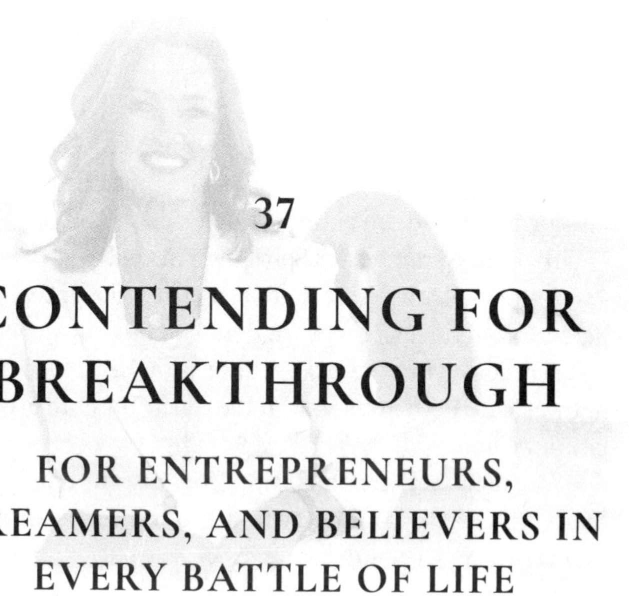

37

CONTENDING FOR BREAKTHROUGH

FOR ENTREPRENEURS, DREAMERS, AND BELIEVERS IN EVERY BATTLE OF LIFE

> *...So, I will go to the king, which is against the law; and if I perish, I perish!*
>
> (Esther 4:16 NKJV).

> *Let us not become weary in doing good, for at the proper time we will reap a harvest if we do not give up*
>
> (Galatians 6:9 NIV).

Breakthrough rarely comes without resistance.

Whether you're believing for business expansion, contending for healing, praying over a loved one, or standing in faith for a financial shift—there will be moments when quitting feels easier than pressing on. But just like Esther, you're not called to shrink back—you're called to stand in the gap and contend.

Esther didn't tiptoe around her calling. She didn't wait for the "right time" or settle for comfort. She fasted. She prayed. And then, she risked everything in obedience to God's timing and purpose. The result? Breakthrough—not just for her, but for an entire nation.

That same courageous Spirit lives in you.

Your small, unseen acts of obedience—the prayer whispered through tears, the work done in faith, the generosity when it costs you, the discipline in slow seasons—they're not wasted. They're weapons in the spirit. They are breaking ground where your eyes can't yet see.

You may feel stretched, tired, or unseen, but Heaven sees you. God is working behind the scenes—even in the silence. Don't let the delay convince you that the promise has died.

Delay is not denial—it's often preparation.

You weren't placed in this moment by accident. You were born for such a time as this. And when you contend with bold, faith-filled obedience, you don't just secure breakthrough for yourself—you unlock it for others, too.

What does it look like to contend for breakthrough?

- Praying even when you feel like quitting.
- Showing up faithfully when no one notices.
- Speaking life in spiritually dry places.
- Sowing generously when you're believing for provision.
- Trusting God's promise, even when the path feels unclear.

PRAYER

Father, thank You that You are the God of breakthrough. Like Esther, give me boldness to move forward in faith, even when I feel uncertain or afraid. Strengthen me when I grow weary and remind me that You are always working—even when I can't see it. Help me not to measure success by speed, but by obedience. I declare that breakthrough is coming—in my business, my family, my health, my finances, and my purpose. Teach me to pray with power, to act with courage, and to wait with hope. In Jesus' name, amen.

JOURNAL QUESTIONS

1. What area of your life are you currently contending for breakthrough in—business, health, family, or faith?
2. Are you approaching it with boldness like Esther, or playing it safe out of fear?
3. What step of faith can you take this week, even if it stretches your comfort zone?

I AM AFFIRMATIONS

I AM a woman of faith, not fear.

I AM contending for breakthrough with boldness and obedience.

I AM aligned with Heaven, and my prayers carry power.

I AM not intimidated by resistance, I am strengthened by grace.

I AM faithful in the battle, and I will see the victory.

I AM acknowledging that I was born for such a time as this.

38

STAY THE COURSE

PURSUING YOUR DREAMS DESPITE DOUBT

Your vision is worth pressing forward, even when others can't see it yet.

"For I know the plans I have for you," declares the Lord, "plans to prosper you and not to harm you, plans to give you hope and a future"

(Jeremiah 29:11 NIV).

Do not be misled: "Bad company corrupts good character"

(1 Corinthians 15:33 NIV).

As a SHE-EO, your dreams are bold. They may feel bigger than what the world around you can comprehend. Sometimes, even the people closest to you may question your vision, doubt your strategy, or struggle to understand your calling.

But here's the truth: your dream doesn't require their approval—it requires your faith and perseverance.

Every trailblazer has faced skepticism. Every innovator has encountered naysayers. Every entrepreneur has wrestled with voices telling them it's impossible. Yet God calls you to move forward—not for applause, but for alignment with His purpose.

Staying the course means:

- Trusting God's timing even when others don't.
- Choosing faith over fear, vision over validation.
- Protecting your energy and your circle from doubt and negativity.
- Remembering that not everyone will understand your journey—and that's okay.

Your dreams are God-given. They carry your influence, legacy, and impact. When you walk faithfully in His direction, the right people, resources, and opportunities will align.

Keep moving. Keep building. Keep leading. Because a SHE-EO doesn't wait for permission—she moves with purpose.

PRAYER

Father, thank You for planting big dreams in my heart. When others doubt, criticize, or fail to understand, remind me that my purpose comes from You—not from their approval. Strengthen my faith, guard my vision, and help me walk confidently in the path You've set for me. Surround me with encouragement, wisdom, and clarity, and give me the courage to rise above skepticism. Let Your plans prosper in my life and use my dreams to glorify You and bless others. In Jesus' name, amen.

JOURNAL QUESTIONS

1. Which voices in my life are discouraging me from pursuing my dreams? Are they aligned with my faith and purpose?
2. Where have I allowed others' doubt to slow me down or shake my confidence?
3. What steps can I take today to protect my vision and stay the course?
4. How can I deepen my trust in God's timing and guidance for my dreams?

I AM AFFIRMATIONS

I AM a SHE-EO walking boldly in the dreams God has given me.

I AM not dependent on the approval of others—I am guided by God's purpose.

I AM steadfast, resilient, and unwavering in pursuit of my calling.

I AM trusting God's timing, plan, and provision for my life and business.

I AM rising above doubt, criticism, and fear, moving forward with faith and courage.

I AM building my legacy, one step at a time, aligned with Heaven's plan.

39

GETTING OUT OF THE GAP CALLED "UNFAIR" OR "GRACE IN THE GAP"

Here's what I want you to do: Find a quiet, secluded place so you won't be tempted to role-play before God. Just be there as simply and honestly as you can manage. The focus will shift from you to God, and you will begin to sense his grace

(Matthew 6:6 MSG).

I have learned how to be content with whatever I have. ...I can do everything through Christ, who gives me strength

(Philippians 4:11-13 NLT).

Life and business aren't always fair. You pour out your heart, sow in faith, and yet sometimes it feels like others are reaping what you've been praying for. That's the *gap*—the space between what you hoped would happen and what seems to be happening.

When you sit in that gap too long, your heart can start to whisper, "It's unfair." But *unfair* is not your final destination. It's an invitation—an invitation to shift your focus from what you can't control to the One who controls it all.

Jesus said in Matthew 6:6 that when we get alone with God—away from the noise, performance, and pressure—our focus shifts. In that secret place, perspective changes. What feels unfair loses its power because you remember that God is still writing your story.

Paul reminds us in Philippians 4 that contentment isn't found in circumstances, but in Christ. Whether the deal closes or the door closes, whether your numbers rise, or resources run low—you *can* do all things through Him who gives you strength.

When you release the need for life or business to feel "fair," you make room for peace, creativity, and faith to flourish. You begin to see that every delay, detour, and disappointment is still working together for your good and God's glory.

You don't live in the gap—you grow through it.

PRAYER

Father, thank You for meeting me in the places that feel unfair. Help me to shift my focus from frustration to faith and from striving to surrender. Teach me to rest in Your presence, knowing You are faithful to complete what You've started. I choose to trust that every "gap" in my story is a place where Your grace will meet me. Fill me with contentment and courage to keep walking in obedience, no matter what I see. In Jesus' name, amen.

JOURNAL QUESTIONS

1. In what areas of my life or business have I been feeling like things are "unfair"?
2. How has that mindset affected my peace, focus, or faith?
3. What might God be teaching or refining in me during this waiting or "gap" season?
4. How can I shift from frustration to faith—from focusing on "unfair" to focusing on God's goodness?
5. What does contentment look like for me right now, in this exact season?

I AM AFFIRMATIONS

I AM at peace, trusting that God is working behind the scenes on my behalf.

I AM no longer trapped by what feels unfair—I am free in Christ's perfect plan.

I AM content, not because everything is easy, but because God is enough.

I AM growing stronger, wiser, and more faithful in the gap.

I AM aligned with Heaven's timing and confident in God's justice and grace.

40

YOU'RE NOT TOO MUCH

YOU'RE DESIGNED FOR THIS

Your multidimensional calling is not a flaw—it's God's design.

She is clothed with strength and dignity, and she laughs without fear of the future

(Proverbs 31:25 NLT).

Somewhere along the way, you may have been told—or at least made to feel—that you're too *much*. Too driven. Too passionate. Too opinionated. Too emotional. Too spiritual. Too loud. Too soft. Too ambitious. Too tender. Like you needed to shrink, tone it down, or choose one lane to be accepted.

But here's the truth: you were never meant to be simple or small. You were designed with depth. With dimension. With a divine mix of strength and sensitivity, leadership and nurture, fire and grace.

Your ability to multitask between boardrooms and bedtime stories or late-night talks with your teens, team strategy and tender prayers, spreadsheets and date nights—it's not a flaw. It's evidence of God's intentional craftsmanship. Ephesians 2:10 says you are His workmanship, His *poema*. A divine poem. A masterpiece made with purpose.

So don't apologize for being multifaceted. Don't minimize your calling to make someone else feel more comfortable. God isn't overwhelmed by your capacity because He created it. Your boldness doesn't cancel out your gentleness. Your dreams don't erase your devotion. Your leadership doesn't disqualify your tenderness.

You don't need to dilute who you are—you need to surrender all of who you are to the One who formed you. Because in His hands, your multidimensional life becomes a multi-impactful calling.

When you live fully as yourself, led by His Spirit, you give other women permission to do the same. Not perfect. Not performing. But whole. So today, instead of asking, "Am I too much?" Ask, "God, how do You want to use everything You put in me?" And then BOLDLY WALK IN IT!

PRAYER

Father, thank You for making me complex, creative, and capable. I lay down the pressure to be less than I am or to hide what You've placed inside me. Teach me to walk confidently in every part of who You created me to be—not with pride, but with surrendered boldness. I choose to stop shrinking and start showing up in the fullness of who You created me to be. In Jesus' name, amen.

JOURNAL QUESTIONS

1. What part of me have I been downplaying to fit in or to avoid criticism?
2. How is God inviting me to own and embrace that part of me today—not for my glory, but for His?

I AM AFFIRMATIONS

I AM not too much, I am God's intentional design.

I AM created with purpose, strength, and beauty.

I AM both visionary and nurturer, both fierce and tender.

I AM fully equipped for every role I've been entrusted with.

I AM not here to shrink, I am here to shine with humility and confidence.

I AM God's workmanship created for purpose and beauty in every area of my life.

I AM walking in the fullness of who I am, and I make no apologies for it.

41

GRATITUDE OVER SATISFACTION

Rejoice always, pray continually, give thanks in all circumstances; for this is God's will for you in Christ Jesus

(1 Thessalonians 5:16-18 NIV).

Enter with the password: "Thank you!" Make yourselves at home, talking praise. Thank him. Worship him!

(Psalm 100:4 MSG)

As a woman of faith and purpose, your calling in business is not only about profit—it's about purpose, impact, and obedience to God's direction. Gratitude is the fuel that keeps that purpose alive.

But here's the truth, many miss—gratitude and satisfaction are not the same thing.

Gratitude gives glory to God for what is, while still believing Him for what will be. Satisfaction, on the other hand, can quietly whisper, "You've done enough. You can settle here."

When we settle, we stop stretching. And when we stop stretching, we stop growing.

Jim Rohn said, "One of the greatest challenges in life is being happy with what you have while in pursuit of what you want." That's the sweet spot of the faith-filled entrepreneur—being thankful for every client, partner, and idea, yet still expectant for the next opportunity God is preparing.

Gratitude keeps your heart soft, your perspective clear, and your energy aligned with divine purpose. It turns every obstacle into an opportunity to witness God's faithfulness.

So today, be grateful but never satisfied. Celebrate progress, not perfection. Let gratitude be your grounding, and growth be your goal.

PRAYER

Heavenly Father, thank You for every blessing You've placed in my hands and every dream still unfolding before me. Teach me to live with a heart full of gratitude, even as I reach for greater things. Let my gratitude glorify You and fuel my growth, that my business would reflect Your goodness in all I do. I surrender my plans, my progress, and my profits to You. May everything I create bring honor to Your name. In Jesus' name, amen.

JOURNAL QUESTIONS

1. What blessings in my business or personal life have I overlooked because I was focused on what's next?
2. Where have I confused satisfaction with gratitude?

3. How can I express more gratitude today while still stretching toward the vision God gave me?
4. If I committed to being just 1 percent better every day, what small changes could I start with?

I AM AFFIRMATIONS

I AM grateful for how far I've come and excited for where God is taking me.
I AM growing daily—in wisdom, in faith, and in purpose.
I AM a vessel of abundance, impact, and grace.
I AM thankful, not complacent.
I AM open to the new opportunities God is preparing for me.
I AM walking in divine purpose and limitless potential.

CLOSING REFLECTION

Gratitude doesn't keep you still; it gives you the strength to keep moving forward with joy. Remember, gratitude opens doors that satisfaction quietly closes. Keep your eyes on the next level God has for you, but never forget to thank Him for the step you're standing on today.

42

CHOOSING WHAT IS BETTER

WALKING AWAY FROM WHAT NO LONGER SERVES YOU

"Martha, Martha," the Lord answered, "you are worried and upset about many things, but few things are needed—or indeed only one. Mary has chosen what is better, and it will not be taken away from her"
(Luke 10:41-42 NIV).

As a SHE-EO, life is full of responsibilities, opportunities, and demands. It can be easy to fall into busyness, believing that doing more is the same as accomplishing more. But busyness is not a spiritual gift. It is often a distraction from God's best and the calling He has placed on your life.

In this Scripture passage in Luke 10, Martha was distracted by work, while Mary chose to sit at Jesus' feet. Mary chose what was better—intimacy with God, focus, and alignment with purpose.

Choosing what is better sometimes requires courage to walk away:

- From commitments that drain your energy without fulfilling your purpose

- From relationships or environments that no longer align with your calling
- From tasks or obligations that crowd out time for reflection, growth, and God's guidance

One of the most important lessons for SHE-EOs is understanding the power of the words "yes" and "no." These are two of the most powerful words you will ever use:

- Saying yes aligns you with God's strategic plan and moves you toward your purpose.
- Saying no protects your focus, your time, and your energy—even if people are offended.

Not everything is part of your God-designed strategic plan, no matter how good it looks. Choosing what is better means discerning, prioritizing, and focusing on what God is calling you to do. Saying no is not rejection—it is wisdom. Saying yes is obedience and alignment.

Learning to love the sound of your feet walking away is a spiritual discipline. It is the art of prioritizing what truly matters, protecting your joy, and safeguarding your legacy.

Remember, saying no to the wrong things is saying yes to God's best.

PRAYER

Lord, help me to recognize the difference between busyness and purpose. Teach me the power of saying yes and no, and give me the courage to walk away from what no longer serves my calling. Help me to focus on what You are specifically calling me to do, aligning my actions with Your strategic plan. Guard my time, energy, and heart so that I may live fully in

Your will and embrace the blessings of saying yes to Your best. In Jesus' name, amen.

JOURNAL QUESTIONS

1. What activities, commitments, or relationships in my life are keeping me busy but not advancing my purpose?
2. Where do I need to emulate Mary and choose what is better?
3. How comfortable am I saying no to opportunities, even if people may be offended?
4. How can I discern whether to say yes or no based on God's strategic plan for my life?
5. What boundaries can I set to protect my time, energy, and focus for what truly matters?

I AM AFFIRMATIONS

I AM a SHE-EO who chooses what is better over what is busy or distracting.

I AM courageous in walking away from people, commitments, and habits that no longer serve my purpose.

I AM intentional with my time, energy, and focus, investing in what advances my God-given calling.

I AM empowered to say no to what does not align with God's strategic plan for my life.

I AM bold in saying yes to what God is calling me to do, trusting His timing and guidance.

I AM free from guilt when I prioritize purpose over busyness or people-pleasing.

I AM learning to love the sound of my feet walking toward freedom, fulfillment, and purpose.

43

NO REGRETS

FULL SAILS TOWARD GOD'S FUTURE

Forget the former things; do not dwell on the past. See, I am doing a new thing! Now it springs up; do you not perceive it? I am making a way in the wilderness and streams in the wasteland

(Isaiah 43:18-19 NIV).

There's a kind of ache that comes not from what we've done, but from what we *didn't* do—the moments we hesitated, the chances we let slip through our fingers, the doors we were too afraid to walk through.

Mark Twain captured this sentiment with such clarity: "Twenty years from now, you will be more disappointed by the things you didn't do than the ones you did. So, throw off the bowlines. Sail away from the safe harbor. Catch the trade winds in your sails."

God echoes this challenge in Isaiah 43:18-19 (NIV), urging His people not to be held hostage by the past: "*Forget the former things; do not dwell on the past. See, I am doing a new thing!*"

Regret thrives where fear reigns, and faith is absent. But we are called to *see,* to perceive the *new* thing God is doing.

To live eyes-forward. To believe that what God has ahead is greater than anything behind. To not just wait for opportunities but *walk in faith* toward them—even when the path looks like a wilderness, even when it feels risky.

The Lord isn't just preparing a path for us. He's also preparing a legacy for our children and the generations to follow. When we choose bold obedience today, we plant seeds of courage and faith in those who come after us. Our willingness to trust God and seize His promises will echo into our family line.

Are you stuck in regret? Paralyzed by the "what ifs" of the past?

Then hear this: God is not done with you. His invitation is still open. Your future is still full of purpose. He is doing a *new* thing, even now.

So, throw off the bowlines. Leave the safe harbor. Trust the One who commands the winds and seas. There's a vast horizon ahead, and God is already there.

PRAYER

Lord, help me to live free from the regrets of yesterday. Give me eyes to see the new things You are doing and a heart bold enough to chase them. Let me not be paralyzed by fear or past mistakes but fueled by Your promises. May my faith today light a path for those who come after me. In Jesus' name, amen.

JOURNAL QUESTIONS

1. Is there something you've been afraid to pursue that you know God is calling you toward?

2. What past regret might be keeping you from seeing the "new thing" God is doing now?
3. How can your choices today shape the faith and future of your children and the generations to come?

I AM AFFIRMATIONS

I AM free from the regrets of my past.
I AM walking boldly into the new thing God is doing in my life.
I AM not paralyzed by fear; I am empowered by faith.
I AM trusting God to guide my steps and chart my course.
I AM courageous enough to leave the safe harbor and pursue His purpose.
I AM planting seeds of faith and courage for the generations that follow.
I AM living eyes-forward, confident that God's best is ahead.
I AM open to God's leading, ready to seize His promises today.
I AM a legacy-builder, walking in obedience, boldness, and vision.
I AM sailing full speed toward God's future, anchored in His love and provision.

44

THEY ARE NOT HOLDING YOU BACK

THEY ARE WHY YOU'RE CALLED

Your family isn't a hindrance to your dreams; they are part of the dream.

The wise woman builds her house, but with her own hands the foolish one tears hers down

(Proverbs 14:1 NIV).

They can urge the younger women to love their husbands and children...to be busy at home, to be kind, and to be subject to their husbands, so that no one will malign the word of God

(Titus 2:4-5 NIV).

In a world that often praises hustle over home and ambition over intimacy, it can feel like your marriage and your children are slowing you down, like they're detours from the destiny God placed in your heart.

But let's get this straight—your husband and your children are not in the way. They are your "why."

They are not distractions from your calling; they are *part of it*. Before the business, before the brand, before the influence—God gave you them. And He doesn't make mistakes.

Your dream is not too big for your family, but it must be built with your family in mind.

We live in a culture that often tells women they must trade in their softness for strength, their tenderness for tenacity, their nurturing for leadership. But in the Kingdom of God, those qualities were never meant to compete; they were always meant to complement.

As women, we must never abandon our God-given gift of femininity and nurturing spirit in pursuit of purpose and success. These traits are not signs of weakness; they are the exact expression of divine strength that the world so desperately needs. Your ability to care deeply, love wholly, and nurture faithfully is not in conflict with your calling; it is part of your anointing.

When you build in a way that allows your marriage and family to come along on the journey, you're not shrinking your dream; you're expanding its foundation.

Your greatest fulfillment will never come from external success alone; it comes from knowing you honored the divine order God designed:

- He called you to love your husband passionately and to be loved passionately by your husband. Embrace that. It's amazing.
- He called you to nurture your children with love and grace.
- He called you to build something that reflects His heart, starting within the four walls of your home.

A thriving business with a crumbling family is not Kingdom success. But a flourishing home that serves as the launchpad for your purpose? That's an impact that echoes into eternity.

You can be both visionary and present, ambitious and anchored, called and connected—because God has given you the grace to do all things through Him.

So instead of seeing your family as something you must "work around," start seeing them as the first audience to your legacy.

PRAYER

Father, thank You for the gift of my husband and children. Help me to build my life, business, and calling in a way that allows my family to grow with me—not apart from me. Teach me to prioritize with Your wisdom and live with Your peace. Let me never forsake the beauty of my femininity or my nurturing spirit in search of success. I want to lead with grace, build with strength, and love with intention. In Jesus' name, amen.

JOURNAL QUESTIONS

1. Have I unintentionally treated my family as a barrier to my dreams instead of part of the calling?
2. In what ways might I be abandoning my feminine, nurturing nature in pursuit of success?
3. How can I invite my family into the journey in meaningful, joy-filled ways while honoring the full expression of who I am as a woman?

I AM AFFIRMATIONS

I AM a woman of purpose who honors the divine order of my calling.

I AM building a life where my marriage and my motherhood flourish alongside my dreams.

I AM not having to choose between family and vision—I carry grace for both.

I AM embracing my God-given femininity and nurturing with strength and wisdom.

I AM creating a legacy that starts at home and flows into the world.

I AM walking in divine alignment—and I am fully equipped for this journey.

SECTION SIX

LEGACY, IMPACT, AND MULTIPLICATION

Weeks 45-52

45

STEWARD THE VISION

PROTECT, REFINE, AND MULTIPLY WHAT GOD GAVE YOU

Legacy is built when vision is not just birthed but nurtured.

Whoever can be trusted with very little can also be trusted with much...

(Luke 16:10 NIV).

The plans of the diligent lead surely to abundance and advantage, but everyone who acts in haste comes surely to poverty

(Proverbs 21:5 AMP).

Now, a person who is put in charge as a manager must be faithful

(1 Corinthians 4:2 NLT).

The vision God gives you is not a sprint—it's a stewardship.

As a faith-filled SHE-EO, you're not just a dreamer or a doer. You're a *steward* of divine ideas, relationships, resources, and influence. That means it's not enough to simply *start* well—you must also *sustain* and *scale* with wisdom and integrity.

Stewardship begins with recognizing that your business, your platform, and even your creativity belong first to God. You are managing His vision, not manufacturing your own. When you embrace that mindset, your decisions shift from reaction to revelation—from hurried hustle to holy strategy.

That's when you start protecting the vision through discernment: guarding your time, your energy, and your circle. You refine it through excellence, allowing God to prune and polish areas that need growth. And you multiply it through delegation and empowerment, trusting others to carry parts of the mission forward.

This is the secret to sustainable success:

- Faith to start.
- Wisdom to steward.
- Humility to scale.

The woman who partners with God in stewardship never runs dry. She learns that divine ideas don't just need creativity, they need consistency. They need systems, strategy, and a surrendered heart that keeps saying, "God, this is Yours."

Remember, it's not just about what you build, but how you *build it.* Your legacy will outlive your hustle.

PRAYER

Father, thank You for trusting me with vision and influence. Teach me to be a wise steward of every-

thing You've placed in my hands. Help me to manage it with integrity, diligence, and humility. Show me how to protect what matters most—my faith, my family, and my focus. Refine what needs refining, prune what needs pruning, and multiply what carries Your anointing. May my business, my leadership, and my legacy reflect Your excellence and grace. In Jesus' name, amen.

JOURNAL QUESTIONS

1. How well am I currently *stewarding* what God has already entrusted to me?
2. Are there areas in my business or personal life where I need more structure, order, or boundaries?
3. How can I refine my systems, habits, or leadership to better sustain growth?
4. What does faithful stewardship look like for me in this season—spiritually, financially, and relationally?

I AM AFFIRMATIONS

I AM a faithful steward of God's vision.

I AM disciplined, diligent, and devoted to excellence.

I AM protecting my peace, my priorities, and my purpose.

I AM refining my systems and strengthening my strategy with wisdom.

I AM building with integrity, leading with humility, and scaling with grace.

I AM trusted with much because I am faithful with little.

I AM creating legacy—not through hustle, but through holy stewardship.

46

A SHE-EO SOWS, REAPS, AND MULTIPLIES

GIVING TO BLESS AND IMPACT

> *"Bring the whole tithe into the storehouse, that there may be food in my house. Test me in this," says the Lord Almighty, "and see if I will not throw open the floodgates of heaven and pour out so much blessing that there will not be room enough to store it"*
>
> (Malachi 3:10 NIV).

> *Remember this: Whoever sows sparingly will also reap sparingly, and whoever sows generously will also reap generously. Each of you should give what you have decided in your heart to give, not reluctantly or under compulsion, for God loves a cheerful giver. And God is able to bless you abundantly, so that in all things at all times, having all that you need, you will abound in every good work*
>
> (2 Corinthians 9:6-8 NIV).

A SHE-EO understands that true abundance is cultivated in giving, not just earning. The law of sowing and reaping is both a spiritual and life principle: what you plant intentionally—whether time, resources, influence, or mentorship—will grow. Sometimes the growth is slow, requiring patience and persistence; other times it multiplies in ways that exceed your imagination.

Honoring God first is foundational. Giving 10 percent of your income is not a loss; it's an act of faith and obedience. It's a declaration that your business, resources, and influence belong to Him, and that you trust His timing and provision. This simple act aligns your heart, your business, and your vision with God's plan, opening the door for blessings you cannot manufacture on your own.

Generosity over busyness is another hallmark of a SHE-EO. It's not enough to give hours or resources without intention. True generosity is thoughtful, strategic, and designed to uplift others. Mentorship, financial support, and sharing opportunities—these are the seeds that create exponential impact.

A SHE-EO also understands that blessing others leads to blessing yourself. When you invest in others, lift communities, and support causes that empower people to rise, you are planting seeds of multiplied favor, influence, and fulfillment. The act of giving expands your platform, multiplies your opportunities, and builds a legacy that endures beyond personal success.

Faith in the process is essential. Sowing requires trust, especially when results are not immediate. God sees the faithfulness behind every seed, every act of generosity, and He multiplies it in perfect timing. Your obedience, patience, and commitment are the keys to a harvest of blessings.

Finally, a SHE-EO recognizes that when good people make good money, they do great things. Wealth and success are not simply for accumulation; they are tools for Kingdom influence and societal impact. The money, resources, and influence you generate can fund initiatives, lift communities, and create lasting change. Your abundance becomes a platform for empowerment, legacy, and multiplying opportunities for others.

Being a SHE-EO is not only about building a business or empire, but also about creating legacy, impact, and influence through intentional generosity. Your success is magnified when others rise alongside you, and your life becomes a testimony that faithfulness, purpose, and generosity multiply impact far beyond what you can see.

PRAYER

> *Lord, thank You for entrusting me with resources, influence, and opportunity. Help me to honor You with the first portion of everything I earn and to give generously to those in need and to causes that lift others. Teach me to sow with intention, love, and faith, knowing that every act of blessing will return in Your perfect timing. Let my life, business, and influence be a testimony that when good people make good money, they do great things. In Jesus' name, amen.*

JOURNAL QUESTIONS

1. How consistently am I honoring God with the first 10 percent of my resources?
2. In what ways can I give generously to help others rise rather than only investing in my own success?
3. Where might I be holding back resources, influence, or opportunities that could bless someone else?
4. How can I cultivate a mindset of abundance rather than scarcity?

5. How can I ensure that the wealth and influence I generate are used for great things and lasting impact?

I AM AFFIRMATIONS

I AM a SHE-EO who understands the law of sowing and reaping.

I AM faithful to honor God with the first 10 percent of my resources.

I AM generous in giving to those in need and in causes that help others rise.

I AM confident that every seed I plant in obedience will yield a harvest.

I AM abundant in resources, influence, and opportunity.

I AM a leader who blesses others and is blessed in return.

I AM a SHE-EO who knows that when good people make good money, they do great things.

I AM living proof that generosity, faith, and purpose multiply impact.

47

PASSING THE BATON

Legacy isn't what you leave behind—it's who you raise up.

And the things you have heard me say in the presence of many witnesses entrust to reliable people who will also be qualified to teach others

(2 Timothy 2:2 NIV).

A good person leaves an inheritance for their children's children, but a sinner's wealth is stored up for the righteous

(Proverbs 13:22 NIV).

Every visionary SHE-EO knows this truth—success is temporary, but *legacy* lasts.

God didn't design you to just build something impressive; He called you to build something that *outlives* you. As a faith-filled woman leading in business, family, and purpose, your greatest measure of success isn't found in your personal achievements—it's found in the people you've empowered to carry the mission forward.

Think about Paul and Timothy. Paul didn't just preach, he *poured.* He invested time, wisdom, and faith into

Timothy, and through that mentorship, the gospel multiplied far beyond Paul's lifetime.

That's legacy leadership.

- It's not just leading people, it's *developing leaders.*
- It's not just handing over tasks, it's *passing on trust.*
- It's not about control, it's about *continuing the mission.*

When you pour into others—your team, your children, your mentees—you're not losing influence, you're *multiplying it.*

A true SHE-EO doesn't fear being replaced; she prepares to be *duplicated.*

So, who are you raising up? Who's watching your faith, your work ethic, your integrity, your courage? Because they're not just observing your success, they're learning your rhythm, your values, your surrender to God.

The legacy you leave won't be built on perfection; it'll be built on the lives you touched, the leaders you raised, and the faith you modeled through the highs and lows.

So, lead with open hands. Share your wisdom. Trust others with what God has entrusted to you.

And when it's time to pass the baton, know that your race is far from over—it's simply multiplying through others who now run because you chose to lead.

PRAYER

Father, thank You for entrusting me with influence, resources, and purpose. Help me to lead with legacy in mind—not just for today, but for generations to come. Show me who I'm called to invest in and empower. Teach me to release control and trust You with the outcome. May my leadership multiply faith, courage, and excellence in others. Let the seeds I plant today bear fruit that impacts families, communities, and nations tomorrow. In Jesus' name, amen.

JOURNAL QUESTIONS

1. Who is God calling me to mentor, train, or raise up in this season?
2. What wisdom or experience can I begin intentionally passing on to others?
3. Do I lead with control or empowerment?
4. What kind of spiritual, emotional, or business legacy am I building for the next generation?

I AM AFFIRMATIONS

I AM a legacy leader raising others to lead with faith and excellence.

I AM pouring out wisdom, and God multiplies the impact.

I AM not afraid to release control; I trust God's timing and direction.

I AM planting seeds of faith, courage, and vision that will outlive me.

I AM allowing my leadership to multiply through others. I lead to empower, not to impress.

I AM passing the baton with purpose, knowing God's mission will continue through those I've poured into.

48

IF THESE WALLS COULD SPEAK

THE SHE-EO'S INTEGRITY

But you, Belshazzar, his son, have not humbled yourself, though you knew all this. Instead, you have set yourself up against the Lord of heaven. ... You praised the gods of silver and gold, of bronze, iron, wood and stone, which cannot see or hear or understand. But you did not honor the God who holds in his hand your life and all your ways. Therefore he sent the hand that wrote the inscription

(Daniel 5:22-24 NIV).

The story of Daniel 5 takes place in Babylon, where King Belshazzar hosted a lavish feast using sacred temple vessels from Jerusalem, praising false gods. During the feast, a mysterious hand appeared, writing on the wall: *"MENE, MENE, TEKEL, PARSIN."*

Daniel interpreted the message in verses 26-28:

- *Mene* – God has numbered your days; your reign and opportunities are limited.
- *Tekel* – You have been weighed on the scales and found lacking; private character matters as much as public success.

- *Parsin (Peres)* – Your kingdom is divided; inconsistency between private and public life brings division and downfall.

That very night, Belshazzar's kingdom fell. The story is a vivid reminder that God sees everything, and public accomplishments are meaningless if private integrity is lacking.

As a SHE-EO, your leadership is visible—your team, clients, and community notice your success. But the walls of your life—home, office, and private moments—tell the real story.

Ask yourself: Would my family be my biggest supporters based on who I am behind closed doors?

If your private life does not align with your public persona, your influence, credibility, and legacy are at risk. Daniel 5 challenges leaders to be consistent, authentic, and faithful in every space—so that private character and public leadership match. True SHE-EO leadership honors God, strengthens family, and inspires others.

PRAYER

Lord, You see all that I do—in public and private. Search my heart, my decisions, and my habits. Help me to lead with integrity, humility, and courage. May my private life reflect the same faithfulness and excellence that my public life displays. May my family, team, and community see a life surrendered fully to You. Let the walls of my life, if they could speak, declare Your glory and my unwavering commitment to live as a true SHE-EO. In Jesus' name, amen.

JOURNAL QUESTIONS

1. If the walls of my home, office, or life could speak, what would they reveal about my true character?
2. Would my family be my biggest supporters based on who I am behind closed doors?
3. Are my private habits, decisions, and faith practices consistent with my public leadership?
4. In what areas of my life and leadership have I been "weighed and found lacking"?
5. What practical steps can I take today to strengthen consistency, integrity, and alignment with God in every area of life?

I AM AFFIRMATIONS

I AM a SHE-EO who leads with integrity and authenticity in all areas of life.

I AM consistent in my private and public actions, thoughts, and decisions.

I AM accountable to God, knowing that private character is the foundation of lasting influence.

I AM a leader my family and community can fully support and admire.

I AM bold, courageous, and fully aligned with God's purpose for my life.

I AM aware that my time, opportunities, and influence are numbered, and I steward them wisely.

I AM living intentionally so that my walls, if they could speak, would testify to faithfulness, excellence, and God's glory.

49

HOT FLASHES OR HOLY FIRE

She is clothed with strength and dignity, and she laughs without fear of the future

(Proverbs 31:25 NLT).

The peace of God [that peace which reassures the heart, that peace] which transcends all understanding, [that peace which] stands guard over your hearts and your minds in Christ Jesus [is yours]

(Philippians 4:7 AMP).

For God has not given us a spirit of fear, but of power and of love and of a sound mind

(2 Timothy 1:7 NKJV).

God is within her, she will not fall...

(Psalm 46:5 NIV).

For women leading, laughing, and living through life's hot seasons—fueled by faith, fanned by grace, and grounded in God's peace.

I knew life was shifting gears when I found myself tearing up over my color-coded calendar—and not one of those colors meant rest. When I was cranking the thermostat down to 62, and whispering, *"Lord, I need peace that surpasses understanding—and maybe a good night's sleep."*

Let's face it, running a business, managing a household, and walking in your calling can feel like juggling holy fire and hot flashes all at once. But even when life heats up, God's still in control of both your calendar *and* your core temperature. He's not fazed by your mood swings, your meltdowns, or the moments you hide in your office with your iced coffee and a prayer. He's right there in the middle of the heat, holding your heart steady when everything else feels like it's melting.

As a SHE-EO navigating leadership, life, and the occasional emotional heatwave, it can feel like you're running two startups—your business and your body. One minute you're strategizing growth, the next you're strategizing peace and sanity. And realizing both require prayer.

But here's the truth: God never asked you to be unshakable on your own. He simply asked you to be anchored in Him. Your emotions may spike like the temperature, your patience may flicker like Wi-Fi in a storm, but His Spirit stays steady. Always.

Every time you choose prayer over panic, gratitude over grumbling, and Scripture over self-doubt, you reclaim your peace. You remind your soul that you're not powered by caffeine or circumstance—you're powered by Christ.

Maybe the heat you feel isn't punishment, maybe it's *purpose.* Maybe it's God refining you, burning off old fears, false identities, and the need to control everything. You're not losing your cool, you're gaining clarity. You're not falling apart, you're being refashioned in fireproof faith.

So when the day feels overwhelming, take a deep breath (preferably near an air vent), whisper a prayer, and laugh a little. You're not just enduring the heat, you're embodying holy fire. Because yes—even Scripture gives us permission to laugh through it.

PRAYER

Lord, when life feels like a furnace, and my emotions ride like a roller coaster, remind me that You are my calm in the chaos. Teach me to lead with laughter, grace, and grounded faith. Let my business, my body, and my heart all align with Your peace. When the fire rises, make it holy. When I feel the heat, let it remind me that You're refining me for a greater purpose. Thank You for the strength to lead, the courage to laugh, and the grace to rest in You. And Lord, thank You for fans, iced coffees, and friends who pray and make us laugh. You really did think of everything. In Jesus' name, amen.

JOURNAL QUESTIONS

1. What emotion or "heat-of-the-moment" reaction tends to derail my peace or focus?
2. What truth from God's Word can I speak over myself when that moment hits?
3. How can I invite God into my leadership—not just my prayer life?
4. How do I define "strength" in this current season of life and leadership?

I AM AFFIRMATIONS

I AM strong, steady, and Spirit-led.
I AM clothed with dignity, not drenched in doubt.
I AM grounded in grace, not guided by my emotions.
I AM a SHE-EO who leads with faith, humor, and holy fire.
I AM not losing control, I'm gaining clarity.
I AM living proof that heat refines, not defines, me.

50

KINGDOM LEGACY

BUILDING BEYOND YOURSELF

Build a business that impacts generations, not just quarters.

We will not hide these truths from our children; we will tell the next generation about the glorious deeds of the Lord, about his power and his mighty wonders

(Psalm 78:4 NLT).

A good person leaves an inheritance for their children's children…

(Proverbs 13:22 NIV).

A SHE-EO's work is bigger than revenue—it's about purpose, impact, and lasting influence. When you build a business with a legacy mindset, you consider not just your bottom line but how your actions affect your family, employees, community, and even the generations that follow.

Legacy-minded leaders create structures that outlast them: mentorship programs, scalable business models, financial stewardship, and family-friendly policies. These leaders also intentionally model integrity, faith, and boldness so their children and employees witness godly entrepreneurship in action.

Think of your business as both a mission and a ministry. Every decision you make—how you hire, how you invest, how you speak—plants seeds of courage, faith, and opportunity. Your legacy will not just be a product or service, but the lives you've touched and empowered along the way.

PRAYER

Lord, help me lead with a legacy mindset. Guide my decisions, partnerships, and strategies so they honor You and serve others. Give me the wisdom and courage to build structures, systems, and habits that empower people beyond myself. May my business and leadership create a ripple effect of faith, opportunity, and purpose that blesses generations to come. In Jesus' name, amen.

JOURNAL QUESTIONS

1. What kind of legacy do I want my business and leadership to leave?
2. How can I create systems that empower others and outlast my direct involvement?
3. Which personal habits or values do I need to strengthen to model godly leadership?
4. How can my daily decisions positively influence the next generation?

I AM AFFIRMATIONS

I AM building a business that leaves a lasting legacy.
I AM intentional in creating impact beyond myself.

I AM using my God-given leadership skills to empower future generations.
I AM making decisions rooted in faith, purpose, and vision.
I AM planting seeds of influence that will flourish for years to come.

51

FAITHFUL FINISH

WELL DONE, SHE-EO

I have fought the good fight, I have finished the race, I have kept the faith

(2 Timothy 4:7 NIV).

His master replied, "Well done, good and faithful servant! You have been faithful with a few things; I will put you in charge of many things. Come and share your master's happiness!"

(Matthew 25:23 NIV)

And don't allow yourselves to be weary or disheartened in planting good seeds, for the season of reaping the wonderful harvest you've planted is coming!

(Galatians 6:9 TPT)

Finishing well isn't about perfection—it's about faithfulness. God isn't asking you to do everything; He's asking you to *stay faithful* to what He's entrusted to you. The true mark of a Kingdom leader isn't how much she achieves, but how deeply she abides and how consistently she obeys.

You've shown up. You've sown, prayed, built, stretched, and believed. Through highs and lows, God has been shaping you into a woman who leads with both purpose and presence.

A faithful finish is not about crossing a finish line in your own strength—it's about *finishing in stride with the Spirit.* God measures success not by how much you've produced, but by how fully you've trusted Him in the process.

Faithful finishing means you can look back without regret and look forward without fear. You know that your obedience has created ripples beyond what you can see. The rooms you built, the teams you led, the people you served—these are all seeds in the soil of eternity.

And as you reach this point in your SHE-EO journey, Heaven whispers over you: "Well done, daughter. You were faithful with what I gave you."

Let that promise be your peace. Let it fuel your next beginning. Because every faithful finish is also the seed of a brand-new start.

PRAYER

Father, thank You for walking with me through every season of this journey. Thank You for reminding me that faithfulness is success in Your eyes. Help me to finish every assignment with excellence, grace, and joy. I lay down the pressure to perform and pick up the posture of peace. I trust that You are pleased not because I've done it all perfectly, but because I kept showing up with You. As I step into what's next, give me fresh fire, renewed vision, and deeper rest in Your presence. Let my life, my leadership, and my legacy bring You glory. In Jesus' name, amen.

JOURNAL QUESTIONS

1. What does "finishing faithfully" look like in this current season of my life or business?
2. Where have I seen God's faithfulness sustain me when I wanted to quit?
3. What am I releasing to God as I close this chapter—and what new beginning is He stirring in me?
4. How can I celebrate what God has done through me, not just what I've achieved?
5. Who can I encourage, mentor, or empower as part of my faithful legacy?

I AM AFFIRMATIONS

I AM finishing strong because God is my strength.
I AM faithful in the little and the large; God trusts me with His vision.
I AM walking in grace, not striving for perfection.
I AM grateful for the growth, not just the goals.
I AM a SHE-EO who leads, loves, and finishes with faith.
I AM ready for the next season because I'm rooted in God's purpose.

52

REFLECTION WEEK

GRATITUDE, REVIEW, AND RENEWAL

Seven-Day Recap
Faithful Then. Faithful Now. Faithful Forever.

The Lord has done great things for us, and we are filled with joy

(Psalm 126:3 NIV).

I have fought the good fight, I have finished the race, I have kept the faith

(2 Timothy 4:7 NIV).

DAY 1: LOOK BACK IN WONDER — THE GOD WHO KEPT YOU

Psalm 77:11 (NIV): "*I will remember the deeds of the Lord; yes, I will remember your miracles of long ago.*"

Before you plan what's next, pause to look back at what God has already done. Every answered prayer, every closed door, every lesson in the wilderness—He was there in it all.

REFLECTIONS

- What are three moments this year when you can clearly see God's hand?
- Write them as *stones of remembrance* in your journal.

PRAYER

Lord, thank You for being constant. When I couldn't see the path, You were still leading. When I didn't feel strong, You were still sustaining. I remember, and I give thanks.

DAY 2: GRATITUDE OVER REGRET — THANKFUL FOR THE STRETCH

1 Thessalonians 5:18 (NIV): "*Give thanks in all circumstances; for this is God's will for you in Christ Jesus.*"

True gratitude transforms how we see our story—it turns pain into purpose and delay into development.

REFLECTIONS

- What situation tested you this year, but ultimately grew your faith?
- How did gratitude shift your perspective?

PRAYER

Father, thank You for the seasons that stretched me. I release regret, comparison, and disappointment. Help me to see Your goodness even in the things I didn't understand.

DAY 3: REVIEW AND RECOGNIZE — ALTARS OF REMEMBRANCE

Joshua 4:7 (NIV): "*...These stones are to be a memorial to the people of Israel forever.*"

Mark the moments when God met you—in stillness, in surrender, in success.

REFLECTIONS

- Revisit each phase of your SHE-EO journey.
- Identify one defining lesson from each season (Identity, Growth, Vision, Leadership, Perseverance, Legacy).

PRAYER

God, You have been faithful in every phase. You turned my confusion into clarity, my weakness into worship. Thank You for every lesson that made me more like You.

DAY 4: RENEW YOUR EYES — STILL CALLED, STILL CHOSEN

Isaiah 6:8 (NIV): *"Then I heard the voice of the Lord saying, 'Whom shall I send?' And I said, 'Here am I. Send me!'"*

The calling didn't expire; your calling is simply evolving. What God began, He intends to complete.

REFLECTIONS

- What is God calling you to continue, and what is He asking you to release?

- Write a fresh "yes" to God—a declaration of surrender and trust.

PRAYER

Here I am, Lord. Renew my heart, sharpen my focus, and align my vision with Yours. I'm still willing, still ready, and still Yours.

DAY 5: REST AND REFUEL — SELAH MOMENTS

Matthew 11:28 (NIV): "*Come to Me, all you who are weary and burdened, and I will give you rest.*"

Rest is not quitting—it's repositioning. You can't pour from an empty vessel; you pour best from overflow.

REFLECTIONS

- How can you create rhythms of rest for the next season?
- What does true rest look like for your soul, not just your schedule?

PRAYER

Jesus, teach me how to rest in Your presence. Quiet the noise, restore my strength, and remind me that my worth isn't in what I produce but in who I belong to.

DAY 6: REFOCUS AND REIMAGINE — VISION RENEWED

Habakkuk 2:2-3 (NKJV): "*…Write the vision and make it plain…. Though it tarries, wait for it; because it will surely come….*"

What God spoke still stands. Now is the time to write again, plan again, and dream again—but this time with refined clarity and renewed courage.

REFLECTIONS

- Rewrite your God-given vision with what you've learned this year.
- What does faithful leadership look like for you now?

PRAYER

Lord, breathe on my vision again. Reignite every dream that honors You. Give me courage to walk into the unknown with faith, not fear.

DAY 7: CELEBRATE AND COMMISSION — FAITHFUL FINISH, FRESH BEGINNING

Philippians 1:6 (NIV): "*...he who began a good work in you will carry it on to completion until the day of Christ Jesus.*"

This isn't the end—it's the continuation of a life led by God. You've finished well because you stayed faithful.

REFLECTIONS

- How will you celebrate what God has done?
- Who can you bless, mentor, or encourage with what you've learned?

PRAYER OF COMMISSION

God, thank You for this journey. I release this year into Your hands and step forward into what's next. Let my life be a testimony of Your faithfulness and my leadership an overflow of Your love. In Jesus' name, amen.

FINAL BLESSING

You've built, stretched, prayed, led, and persevered. Now you stand as a *SHE-EO refined by fire, rooted in grace, and released in purpose.*

May your next season carry the fruit of every seed planted this year. May your influence multiply, your rest deepen, and your faith remain unshakable.

Well done, SHE-EO—you have finished this year faithfully.

Now rise and build again.

Bonus Devotion

STRENGTH FOR THE ASSIGNMENT

SHE-EO TEMPLE CARE ACTION PLAN

A Practical Guide to honoring the body God entrusted to you.

WHY TEMPLE CARE MATTERS FOR THE SHE-EO

You are not just maintaining your body—you are sustaining your mission.

Every Kingdom assignment requires energy, clarity, focus, and endurance. That means physical stewardship is not an optional part of your calling; it is a foundational part of your obedience. You cannot carry spiritual weight in a weary or neglected vessel.

This action plan turns the devotion "Strength for the Assignment" into a lifestyle, not just a moment of inspiration.

This is your blueprint for aligning your body with your purpose.

PART ONE: MINDSET RESET

SHIFTING HOW YOU SEE YOUR BODY

Before you take action, you must confront your beliefs.

1. RENAME YOUR WHY

Replace "I need to get in shape" with:

- "I am preparing my body to carry God's vision."
- "I am strengthening my temple for my assignment."

2. REJECT THE LIES

Say NO to:

- "I don't have time."
- "I'll start next week."
- "This is self-indulgent."
- "This isn't spiritual."

And replace with truth:

- "My health is part of my calling."
- "Discipline is worship."

3. REFRAME MOVEMENT

You're not "working out."

- You're training for purpose.
- You're cultivating longevity.
- You're building capacity.

PART TWO
THE SHE-EO TEMPLE CARE PILLARS

These four pillars form the foundation of your physical stewardship.

PILLAR 1 — MOVEMENT (STRENGTH + MOBILITY)

Goal: 3–5 days a week of intentionally strengthening your body.

- Strength training
- Walking or running
- Stretching/mobility
- Pilates or Barre
- Resistance bands

Purpose: Build endurance to sustain your calling.

PILLAR 2 — NOURISHMENT (FUEL FOR ASSIGNMENT)

Goal: Eat like someone preparing for longevity.

- Prioritize whole, living foods
- Hydrate first, caffeinate second
- Reduce sugar and heavy, draining meals
- Add foods that support energy and focus
- Prioritize protein

Purpose: Fuel the body that carries your vision.

PILLAR 3 — REST (RECOVERY + RESET)

Goal: 7–8 hours of restorative sleep.

Busyness is not a spiritual gift. However, rest is a spiritual discipline. Jesus slept. Elijah slept. God commanded the Sabbath.

Purpose: Recharge the vessel so you do not burn out in the battle.

PILLAR 4 — BOUNDARIES (PROTECTION OF ENERGY)

Goal: Create limits that prevent depletion.

- Limit access to draining people
- Schedule margin
- Say "no" without guilt
- Protect your emotional health

Purpose: Guard the temple to preserve the mission.

PART THREE WEEKLY TEMPLE CARE ACTION PLAN

Use this as a simple, repeatable weekly rhythm.

WEEKLY COMMITMENT OVERVIEW

1. MOVEMENT

✓ 3 intentional strength or movement sessions.
✓ 1 long walk/stretch session.
✓ 1 rest day.

2. NOURISHMENT

✓ Plan 2 or 3 balanced meals each day.
✓ Drink water before your morning coffee.
✓ Meal prep one batch meal for busy days.

3. REST

✓ Commit to a bedtime.
✓ One evening a week with no screens.
✓ A weekly Sabbath pause.

4. BOUNDARIES

✓ One "No" that protects your peace.
✓ One hour of personal care (bath, journal, massage, skincare, silence).
✓ One moment to evaluate emotional health.

WEEKLY CHECK-IN QUESTIONS

Use these every Sunday:

1. What drained me this week?
2. What nourished me?
3. Did I honor my body or ignore it?
4. Where did I choose discipline over feelings?
5. What adjustments must I make for next week?

PART FOUR
30-DAY TEMPLE CARE CHALLENGE

Use this if you want to elevate the action plan into a short-term spiritual commitment.

DAILY NON-NEGOTIABLES

- Move your body for 15+ minutes.
- Drink water before any other beverage.
- Eat one intentionally nourishing meal.
- Go to bed at a consistent time.
- Speak one "I AM" affirmation aloud.

WEEKLY NON-NEGOTIABLES

- One longer workout or walk.
- One meal prepared ahead of time.
- One rest/reset moment.
- One journal reflection.
- One boundary reinforced.

PART FIVE
SHE-EO TEMPLE CARE PRAYER

Lord, thank You for the body You entrusted to me. Strengthen me to honor this temple with wisdom and discipline. Teach me to see my health as holy, my movement as worship, and my choices as stewardship. Give me the grace to build strength for my assignment—physically, mentally, and spiritually. Empower me to choose purpose over preference and longevity over convenience. Let my habits honor You. Let my energy glorify You. Let my body be a vessel worthy of the calling You placed within me. In Jesus' name, amen.

PART SIX
FINAL AFFIRMATION

SHE-EO TEMPLE DECREES

- I honor the temple God gave me.
- I fuel the body that carries my calling.
- I am building strength for the assignment ahead.
- I choose discipline over feelings.
- I am committed to longevity, clarity, and vitality.
- My health is worship.
- My wellness is obedience.
- My body is a vessel of purpose, and I care for it with intention.

CLOSING THOUGHTS

Your body is not an afterthought—it is part of God's blueprint.

Caring for your temple is caring for your calling.

A SHE-EO doesn't just strengthen her mind and spirit; she strengthens the vessel that carries both.

This action plan isn't about perfection—it's about consistency. Small steps today build the endurance you will need tomorrow.

Your assignment deserves a healthy, energized, disciplined YOU.

ABOUT KAREN SCHATZLINE

Karen Schatzline is an international Christian evangelist and author who, together with her husband, Pat Schatzline, founded Remnant Ministries International in 1997. For more than two decades, she has ministered with passion, bold faith, and prophetic fire, delivering messages that bring hope, freedom, and a deep call to intimacy with the Father.

Through her preaching, writing, and television appearances, Karen has reached millions around the world with a powerful message of God's love, the freedom found in Christ, and the authority believers carry to overcome the lies of the enemy. Her ministry is marked by authenticity, spiritual depth, and a strong emphasis on transformation from the inside out.

Karen is the author of *Dehydrated* and, alongside her husband, co-author of *Rebuilding the Altar* and *Restore the Roar*—a compelling book on defeating fear through the breath and power of God. She is also the author of her newest book, *Becoming SHE-EO*, which guides women through a yearlong journey of becoming all God created them to be.

In addition to her writing and preaching ministry, Karen leads a widely followed video vlog called "The Breathing Room," which has ministered to tens of thousands by helping people pause, breathe deeply, and encounter God in life-giving, practical ways.

She is also the founder and leader of SHE-EO, a powerful women's movement designed to create a Christ-centered community where women encourage, equip, and empower one another to thrive—in their personal lives, marriages and families, and in ministry and business.

Through SHE-EO, Karen hosts online gatherings and events that impact thousands of women worldwide, particularly faith-filled entrepreneurs and CEOs.

Together with her husband, Pat, Karen co-founded a health-coaching company in 2016 that has helped tens of thousands of people begin living healthier, more vibrant lives—spiritually, emotionally, and physically.

Karen and Pat make their home in Fort Worth, Texas. They are the proud parents of two adult children, Abby Schatzline, a 23-year-old brilliant marketing major, and Nate Schatzline, who serves as the District 93 Texas State House Representative. Nate and his wife, Adrienne, have also made Karen and Pat the joyful grandparents of three beautiful grandchildren: Jackson, Anderson, and Skylar.

WEBSITE AND SOCIAL MEDIA:

RAISETHEREMNANT.COM
SCHATZLINESBOOKS.COM
Instagram: @Karenschatzline
Facebook: (Ministry) www.facebook.com/KarenSchatzline
Facebook: (Personal) www.facebook.com/kschatzline
YouTube:
www.youtube.com/RemnantMinistriesInternational

REFLECTIONS

DREAMS AND GOALS

Join the Movement

www.sheeomovement.com

Schedule Karen

raisetheremnant.com/schedule

Connect with Karen

Instagram: @karenschatzline

Facebook: KarenSchatzline

X: @KarenSchatzline

REMNANT MINISTRIES

Evangelists Pat and Karen Schatzline co-lead & formed Remnant Ministries International, an evangelistic ministry, in 1997 to awaken the remnant and call people of all ages back to an encounter with God.

With a schedule that stays full year-round, Pat and Karen travel nationally and internationally, ministering a message of hope, purpose and healing.

They are the authors of several books: "Why Is God So Mad at Me?", "I Am Remnant", "Dehydrated", "Unqualified" "Rebuilding the Altar" and "Restore the Roar".

Connect with Pat & Karen:

Instagram: @patschatz @karenschatzline

Facebook:
facebook.com/PatSchatzline
facebook.com/KarenSchatzline

X: @Patschatz @KarenSchatzline

www.raisetheremnant.com

In the Right Hands, This Book Will Change Lives!

Most of the people who need this message will not be looking for this book. To change their lives, you need to **put a copy of this book in their hands.**

Our ministry is constantly seeking methods to find the people who need this anointed message to change their lives. **Will you help us reach these people?**

Extend this ministry by sowing three, five, ten, or *even more* books today and change people's lives for the better! Your generosity will be part of catalyzing the Great Awakening that many have been prophesying and praying for.

YOUR Prophetic COMMUNITY

Sign up for a **FREE** subscription to the Destiny Image digital magazine and get awesome content delivered directly to your inbox!

destinyimage.com/signup

Sign up for Cutting-Edge Messages that Supernaturally Empower You

- Gain valuable insights and guidance based on biblical principles
- Deepen your faith and understanding of God's plan for your life
- Receive regular updates and prophetic messages
- Connect with a community of believers who share your values and beliefs

Experience Fresh Video Content that Reveals Your Prophetic Inheritance

- Receive prophetic messages and insights
- Connect with a powerful tool for spiritual growth and development
- Stay connected and inspired on your faith journey

Listen to Powerful Podcasts that Propel You into God's Presence Every Day

- Deepen your understanding of God's prophetic assignment
- Experience God's revival power throughout your day
- Learn how to grow spiritually in your walk with God